*Recent Middle
English Scholarship
And Criticism:
Survey And
Desiderata*

RECENT

Middle English

Scholarship

and

Criticism:

Survey and Desiderata

Edited by   J. BURKE SEVERS

Duquesne University Press, Pittsburgh, Pa.
Editions E, Nauwelaerts, Louvain

First Printing

Library of Congress catalog card number: 76–107357

Standard Book Number: 8207–0131–9

PRINTED IN THE UNITED STATES OF AMERICA

Preface

The four essays in this little volume in their original form were delivered as papers before the Chaucer and Middle English Groups of the Modern Language Association between Christmas 1968 and New Year's Day 1969, when Donald Howard and I, respectively, were chairmen of the two Groups. The Association's Committee on Research Activities had recommended that the meetings this year give attention to a reassessment in detail of the state of research in each Group; and these papers were intended to supply the need for a survey of recent scholarship and criticism, with especial notice of desiderata, in certain major areas of Middle English literature. From the first it was intended that the papers by David Fowler, Donald Howard, and Lillian Hornstein be published together; and when I heard Helaine Newstead's paper at the Chaucer Group, I realized at once that it was a perfect companion and complement to the other three papers, and I prevailed upon her, with Chairman Howard's consent, to permit it to be published with them.

The essays are the product of four of the most eminent Middle English scholars. All are well-known experts treating of areas in which they have special competence — areas, indeed, to which they have made important contributions. The depth and range of their knowledge have enabled them to identify and evaluate recent trends, occasionally even to make fresh contributions in these essays, often to point out clearly what we do not

5

know and where future research will be most fruitful. Considerable controversy swirls around some islands in these seas, and the fact that our essayists have been involved in these controversies gives special piquancy and special significance to their reports, though I think that even their scholarly opponents will agree that they have sought honestly to maintain appropriate scholarly objectivity and fairness of judgment.

Rarely has there been a time when the sort of guidance which these essays provide was more urgently needed. We are beset by false prophets and by prophets who, with only partial and clouded insight, are uttering strange gospel to the faithful. May these essays help shed light rather than darkness around our feet.

J. Burke Severs
Lehigh University
April 15, 1969

Contents

Piers Plowman

by David C. Fowler

Thirty years have passed since Morton Bloomfield wrote his review of *Piers Plowman* studies, and in that time there have been important developments in the interpretation of this major Middle English poem which I will try to describe. I ask forgiveness in advance, however, if my survey seems less balanced and objective than Bloomfield's. He composed his review calmly before entering the fray; I write as an embattled participant in the intense, exhilarating conflict now taking place on the darkling plain of *Piers Plowman* scholarship.[1]

The decade of the nineteen-forties was a time of transition for *Piers Plowman* studies. The era of the authorship controversy was drawing to a close, and with it the careers of Manly, Knott, Chambers and Grattan, chief participants in a dispute that had raged sporadically since almost the beginning of the twentieth century. Manly, who had started the controversy in 1906, dropped out of it after 1910, in the belief that no further progress could be made until reliable new editions of the three texts could be prepared. Ironically, separate projects for the editing of the A-text by Knott and by Chambers and Grattan were still incomplete when World War II, for a time, forced scholars to put aside their studies.

When I was first introduced to *Piers Plowman* in a seminar with J. R. Hulbert at Chicago in 1947, work on the poem seemed to be virtually at a standstill. Occasional explorations of text and manuscript problems by Mitchell, Bennett, Grattan, and Kane were appearing,[2] and echoes of the authorship controversy survived in articles by Chambers, Huppé, and Stroud.[3] Aside from Father Dunning's excellent book on the A-text, however, which had been published in 1937, there was little on the horizon to suggest what might be the new direction of *Piers Plowman* studies.[4] Meanwhile, a few important articles appeared. Dunning corrected Chambers in the matter of the righteous heathen, Coghill delivered a suggestive lecture on levels of meaning in the poem, Gerould put his *imprimatur* on earlier efforts to make sense of the structure of the B-text, and Hulbert drew up an angry indictment of Chambers' published work on *Piers Plowman.*[5]

Faced with these alarms and excursions, I chose as my first effort in this area an edition of the A-text, which was published in 1952, thus bringing to completion the project begun many years ago by the late Thomas A. Knott.[6] Meanwhile, the editorial torch of Chambers and Grattan was passed on to George Kane, who had been Chambers' student in the University of London, and who, after World War II, headed a group of British and American scholars dedicated to the task of publishing an edition of all three versions of the poem.[7] Kane's edition of the A-text was published in 1960, and it is hoped that the B-text will appear before long, and the C-text sometime in the next decade.[8] These volumes, when completed, will no doubt become the definitive edition of *Piers Plowman* in this century.

Turning now from textual to literary studies, it should be said, first, that the "modern" period of *Piers Plowman* criticism begins with Donaldson's book on the C-text, published in 1949.[9] In addition to being carefully researched and full of valuable information, this study is a pleasure to read. After twenty years, it is still an important book for anyone interested in the poem. The main obstacle for Donaldson in writing it, I feel sure, was the fact that he chose the latest form of the poem, the C-text, as his subject, at a time when even the B-text remained largely an enigma. Hence very often, in writing about C, Donaldson had first to set forth his interpretation of the parallel passage of B before attempting to give his interpretation of the C-text. This, plus the acknowledged textual uncertainties, made his task extremely difficult. Yet his boldness in this regard resulted in a very valuable book, and probably was a factor in encouraging others to follow his lead.

Equally important for the future of *Piers Plowman* studies was the book by Robertson and Huppé, *Piers Plowman and Scriptural Tradition*, published two years later in 1951. Despite the criticism of this volume by Donaldson and others, I find myself decisively on the side of Kaske and those who regard it as a major pioneering work in exegetical criticism, a field of growing importance in medieval studies over the past two decades. The protests of literary critics against the Robertsonian school are not, I think, entirely an expression of righteous indignation over its apparent shortcomings in aesthetic analysis. They also contain an oblique acknowledgement of Robertson's exposure of a tendency toward condescension in much modern criticism of the literature of the Middle Ages. Even a slight trace of condescension in the mind of a critic, no matter how sensitive he is to literature, can impeach his critical conclusions. Robertson's scholarship, his profound knowledge of and respect for medieval thought, are, I think, having a salutary effect in the field of medieval studies.

The decade of the fifties was a period of rapid increase in *Piers Plowman* studies, coming not only from the post-war pioneers already mentioned, but also from younger scholars destined to make significant contributions in the future. I refer to such people as Burrow, Frank, Kaske, Lawlor and Salter. Burrow is especially knowledgeable in the poetry of the alliterative revival, and has commented perceptively on the poetic diction of *Piers* in his discussion of "secondary ironic effects," included in an article entitled "The Audience of *Piers Plowman*" which appeared in 1957.[11]

Kaske has been engaged in a conscious and deliberate effort to provide the kind of in-depth analysis and documentation of the poem needed to validate the generalizations of Robertson and Huppé, but without surrendering his own point of view in the process.[12] The depth of learning and the passionate pursuit of solutions that are characteristic of Kaske's half dozen articles on *Piers* have led one colleague to call him a "crux-buster," an epithet which I dare mention because I think it expresses at least as much admiration as it does criticism.

John Lawlor and Elizabeth Salter have that wide-ranging yet thorough knowledge of literature which is characteristic of British scholarship, together with a particular interest in *Piers Plowman* expressed in significant articles and books in the nineteen-fifties and early sixties.[13] The fact that Lawlor gives his volume the subtitle "An Essay in Criticism," and Mrs. Salter calls her book "An Introduction," reminds us that both are addressing the non-specialist interested in literature of all periods. The publication of books of this type is to some extent a sign of success for *Piers Plowman* studies, but we can be particularly grateful that the authors in this case happen also to be critics with solid, scholarly knowledge of the poem.[14]

By far the most important study to appear in the fifties, in my opinion, was the book by R. W. Frank, Jr., *Piers Plowman and the Scheme of Salvation*, published in 1957. The subject of the book is that complex portion of the B-text sometimes called the *Vita*, or *Dowel, Dobet, and Dobest* (B passus VIII-XX). Frank finds that this part of the poem is a unified whole and that it presents the "scheme of salvation," that is, God's plan for the salvation of mankind. His observations on the flexibility of the poet's use of the triad (*Dowel, Dobet, and Dobest*), his rejection of the autobiographical method of reading the poem (still surprisingly popular),[15] and his application to the text of current controversial issues (the friars, penance, and the doctrine of *redde quod debes*), are all very illuminating. But Frank's most salutary contribution was his refutation of the "three lives" theory. I have never thought that *Piers Plowman* has anything whatever to do with the active, contemplative, or mixed lives. Yet this idea had dominated *Piers Plowman* criticism since the work of Wells and Coghill in the early thirties,[16] and was probably still exerting a hypnotic effect on those of us who were then seeking new solutions to the structural problems of the B-text. Certainly Frank's book had a liberating impact, and is no doubt to some extent responsible for the substantial progress that has been made in the last ten years.[17]

The present decade got off to a fast start with the publication of five books in three years: Kane's edition of the A-text in 1960, followed by my comparative study of the A- and B-texts in 1961, and then no fewer than three books in 1962 — the two already mentioned by Lawlor and Salter, and a third long-

13

awaited study by Bloomfield, *Piers Plowman as a Fourteenth-Century Apocalypse.*[18]

My impression of Bloomfield's book is similar to the opinion expressed earlier about Robertson and Huppé's *Piers Plowman and Scriptural Tradition.* Both books are pioneers in the field, while perhaps for that very reason both are open to criticism. I have elsewhere given my detailed evaluation of Bloomfield's study, and therefore will not restate it here.[19] Suffice it to say that he places the poem in a context of monastic tradition that is very enlightening. Undoubtedly the most stimulating discussion is in Chapter IV, "History, Social Theory, and Apocalyptic in *Piers Plowman.*" Here Bloomfield makes effective use of the contrast between the Greek and the Judaeo-Christian traditions in his discussion of the mystic way of individual salvation in contrast to the apocalyptic way of the salvation of society. It is in this ideological sense, I believe, that he makes his best case for *Piers Plowman* as a fourteenth-century apocalypse.

At times I have wondered how it is possible to feel indebted to both Robertson and Bloomfield, as I do, when they differ so decisively with each other.[20] But the reason, I think, is that Robertson's view of the Middle Ages is Hellenistic, in that he sees medieval thought in repose, consisting of stable categories, while Bloomfield's view is Hebraic, seeing medieval thought as dynamic and in motion, with the thrust of history behind it. There is truth in both views, and we are fortunate to have them represented by two of the most learned and distinguished scholars in the medieval field.

The escalation of *Piers Plowman* studies in the nineteen sixties is awesome indeed, and the nearer we approach the present year in our survey the more difficult it becomes to do justice to the many projects now at various stages of completion and publication. Well over a dozen American graduate students

14

have written dissertations on the poem in the last eight years, and three of these, John F. Adams, Ben H. Smith, and Edward Vasta, have issued some of their findings in published form.[21] The quality of their work is excellent, and holds promise of significant contributions to come.

Meanwhile, overseas in England, three new students, Kean, Spearing, and Woolf, are turning out important articles. In addition to a valuable comparative review of the the two modern editions of the A-text, Miss Kean has published articles explicating concepts in the B-text that are both learned and illuminating.[22] Spearing has not only written perceptively on imagery in *Piers Plowman*, he has also produced an important book, *Criticism in Medieval Poetry*, which seeks to bring the precepts of the new criticism to bear in a study of representative works of fourteenth-century English poetry.[23] I have seen only one article by Miss Woolf on *Piers Plowman*, but that an important one to which I refer again in a moment.

Now that we have reached the present day in our survey, it is tempting to look for that cloud on the horizon, no bigger than a man's hand, which is a portent of things to come. I have succumbed to this temptation, and am persuaded that I see such a sign in recent articles by Woolf, Burrow, and Muscatine.[24] What these three studies have in common, despite the differences in their subjects, is a concern for discovering what Burrow calls the "ground-plan" of the poet, together with a conviction that this complex and tortuous poem expresses a loss of faith in the traditional values of medieval man.

Miss Woolf alludes in her article to the "lack of a sustained literal level" in the poem, a problem which I believe lies at the root of the difficulty that scholars have had in perceiving the structure of the B-text. It is possible to argue, for example, that the literal level of the B-continuation is based on a progression through the Bible, from Genesis to Revelation.[25] But it is indeed difficult to perceive this, particularly in the first five passus of the continuation, where the literal level is concealed in a dazzling series of digressions, each with its own carefully designed function as a corrective to ideas embodied in the A-text. In fact, the structure of the A-text itself is much more readily discernible, as Burrow has shown in his definition of the sequence of the *Visio*, part two, as consisting of sermon, confession, pilgrimage, and pardon. It is to be hoped that he will extend his analysis to the rest of the poem, and to the B-text as well.[26]

In a modest but important article entitled "Locus of Action in Medieval Narrative,"[27] Charles Muscatine has set forth what I consider to be the best single prospectus for future study of *Piers Plowman* that we now have. He calls the shifting locus of action in *Piers* "surrealistic," and he concludes that "the episodes, fragmentary in relation to one another, suggest shorings, passionately and hastily assembled — from heaven or earth — against some impending ruin."[28] The crisis of confidence reflected in the structure of the poem is seen against a background of "Gothic" tension between naturalism of detail and schematization of spatial environment in late medieval art. This remarkable assessment of *Piers Plowman* as a work of art and an expression of the agony of its age (and, by implication, our own) is so full of insight, and so lacking in condescension, that I feel impelled to express the hope that Muscatine will absent himself a while from student unrest, and turn his attention once more to the study of *Piers* begun so auspiciously in this brief article.

In the present survey of *Piers Plowman* scholarship since 1940 I have tried to maintain enough objectivity to justify adding a few subjective remarks of my own at the end. Even if you feel that my efforts in this regard have been without notable success, I trust that there will be no strenuous objection to the following suggestions for future study of the poem.

More than once in the past I have tried to warn against the unfortunate effects of the biographical method of reading *Piers Plowman*, a tendency which I refer to as "Langland harmonistics." My hope is that scholars in the future will become increasingly aware of this danger, and will be scrupulous in treating the three texts of the poem as separate entities. The great care taken in this regard by R. W. Frank was, I think, an important factor in the success of his book, and I commend it as a model for future criticism. A synoptic interpretation, of course, will eventually be necessary, but it will not be possible until the critic has learned to keep all three versions separately and distinctly in mind.

There can be no doubt that the current trend toward emphasis on expounding the traditional nature of thought and imagery in *Piers Plowman* is useful for a better understanding of the work as a whole. At the same time, I believe that more of an effort should be made to see the poem in its immediate historical context. To illustrate this point, I will now provide a hypothetical description of the historical significance of all three texts, with the hope that someone will come along and confirm the accuracy of my hypothesis, or disprove it.

The A-text of *Piers Plowman* was composed between 1362 and 1365, and became almost immediately a very popular poem, circulating widely throughout England. It was written with an undertone of prophetic anger, arising from the injustices generated by social conditions in that restless time. Consequently, it had a great popular impact, with its ringing condemnation of the corrupt establishment and its elevation of the humble plowman to something approaching a messianic role in the renewal of society. Without doubt it was the A-text that fired the leaders of the peasants' revolt, and it is the A-text which is quoted by John Ball in his famous letter to the commons of Essex.

The B-text was composed between 1378 and 1383 (a considerable portion of it *after* the Peasants' Revolt of 1381), with a wide circulation in the intellectual community, particularly Oxford University, but with less national popularity than the A-text had enjoyed. If the A-text was written in anger, the B-text was composed in an agony of spirit over the spectacle of a Christian society divided against itself. The A-text, written by a radical, is impelled forward by the spirit of truth, sharp and judgmental; the B-text, written by a conservative, combines a spirit of charity and forgiveness with a stern rebuke to those who, in their impatience, resort to violence and thus sin against the Holy Ghost. The longer poem ends, paradoxically, in despair and hope: at that moment when God's plan calls for man to do his best, we see him in the final scenes doing his worst.

The C-text was probably written in the early nineties, and represents a revision by the B-poet partly out of an affection for the poem and a desire for its improvement, but more importantly in order to re-appraise and revise what he has to say about issues of social and religious reform. A fresh study of the C-text done with this historical awareness should produce interesting results, analogous to, though not identical with, those achieved so brilliantly by V. H. Galbraith in his essay on Thomas Walsingham and the Saint Albans Chronicle.[29]

Study of *Piers Plowman* from the point of view of imagery and the history of ideas is valuable, but it is really only a preliminary phase which should lead us eventually to an engagement with the poem in its historical setting. G. Ernest Wright, speaking of the Bible, uses a suggestive phrase when he refers to the scholar's responsibility to "walk from the biblical text out into history."

This dictum applies with great force to the study of *Piers Plowman*, a poem written in a time of riots, burnings, and assassinations.[30] Until we learn to walk from our text out into history, we will be in danger of missing the important message which this profound and troubling poem offers to twentieth-century man.

Notes

1. Morton W. Bloomfield, "Present State of *Piers Plowman* Studies," *Speculum,* XIV (1939), 215-232. My own publications relating to *Piers Plowman* are as follows: "Contamination in Manuscripts of the A-Text of *Piers the Plowman,*" *PMLA,* LXVI (1951), 495-504; ed., with T. A. Knott, *Piers the Plowman: A Critical Edition of the A-Version* (Baltimore, 1952); "The Relationship of the Three Texts of *Piers the Plowman,*" *MP,* L (1952), 5-22; "The 'Forgotten' Pilgrimage in *Piers the Plowman,*" *MLN,* LXVII (1952), 524-526; and *Piers the Plowman: Literary Relations of the A and B Texts* (Seattle, 1961). Of interest in connection with my theory of authorship are the following: "John Trevisa and the English Bible," *MP,* LVIII (1960), 81-98; "The Date of the Cornish *Ordinalia,*" *MS,* XXIII (1961), 91-125, and "New Light on John Trevisa," *Traditio,* XVIII (1962), 289-317. In the present survey I also make use of my own reviews of recent books on *Piers Plowman:* review of *Piers Plowman and the Scheme of Salvation,* by R. W. Frank, Jr., and *William Langlands "Piers Plowman": Eine Interpretation des C-Textes,* by Willi Erzgraber, in *MLQ,* XX (1959), 285-287; review of *Piers Plowman: The A Version,* ed. George Kane, in *MP,* LVIII (1961), 212-214; review of *Piers Plowman as a Fourteenth-Century Apocalypse,* by Morton W. Bloomfield, in *MLQ,* XXIV (1963), 410-413; and finally, a review of *Piers Plowman: The Evidence for Authorship,* by George Kane, in *ELN,* III (1966), 295-300.

2. A. G. Mitchell, "A Newly Discovered MS of the C-Text of

Piers Plowman," MLR, XXXVI (1941), 243 ff.; J. A. W. Bennett, "The Date of the A-Text of *Piers Plowman,"* PMLA, LVIII (1943), 566 ff.; the same, "The Date of the B-Text of *Piers Plowman,"* MÆ, XII (1943), 55 ff.; the same, "Lombards' Letters," MLR, XL (1945), 309 ff.; the same, "A New Collation of a *Piers Plowman* Manuscript [HM 137]," MÆ, XVII (1948), 21 ff.; J. H. G. Grattan, "A Newly Discovered Manuscript and Its Affinities [Chaderton, A-Text]," MLR, XLII (1947), 1 ff.; the same, "The Text of *Piers Plowman*: Critical Lucubrations with Special Reference to the Independent Substitution of Similars," SP, XLIV (1947), 593 ff.; George Kane, "Problems and Methods of Editing the B-Text," MLR, XLIII (1948), 1 ff.

3. R. W. Chambers, "Robert or William Langland?" *London Mediaeval Studies,* I (1948 for 1939), pp. 430-462; B. F. Huppé, "The Authorship of the A and B Texts of *Piers Plowman,"* Speculum, XXII (1947), 578-620; T. A. Stroud, "Manly's Marginal Notes on the *Piers Plowman* Controversy," MLN, LXIV (1949), 9-12

4. T. P. Dunning, *Piers Plowman: An Interpretation of the A-Text* (London, 1937). I take this opportunity to call attention to a modestly written but excellent article by Stella Maguire, "The Significance of Haukyn, *Activa Vita,* in *Piers Plowman,"* RES, XXV (1949), 97-109 Unfortunately, I believe she has not published anything more on the subject.

5. T. P. Dunning, "Langland and the Salvation of the Heathen," MÆ, XII (1943), 45-54; N. K. Coghill, "The Pardon of *Piers Plowman"* (Sir Israel Gollancz Memorial Lecture), *British Academy Proceedings,* XXXI (1945); G. H. Gerould, "The Structural Integrity of *Piers Plowman* B," SP, XLV (1948), 60 ff.; and J. R. Hulbert, *"Piers the Plowman* after Forty Years," MP, XLV (1948), 215-225. I am indebted to Mr. Hulbert in many ways, not least for his skeptical attitude in the face of a growing consensus for single authorship. It was his firm,

unfanatical skepticism that enabled me to regard the multiple authorship theory as a live possibility, thus leading eventually to my present theory of dual authorship (A-BC).

6. A by-product of my textual studies was an article on the relationship of the three texts in *Modern Philology* already referred to (note 1 above). In it I argue that certain changes made in the B-text (and preserved in C) appear to be not authorial, but scribal, and should not be attributed to the poet himself. Exception was taken to these conclusions by E. T. Donaldson, "The Texts of *Piers Plowman*: Scribes and Poets," *MP*, L (1953), 269-273, and by A. G. Mitchell and G. H. Russell, "The Three Texts of *Piers the Plowman*," *JEGP*, LII (1953), 445-456. Speaking objectively, I would call this argument a stand-off; the problem is still there, and a solution needs to be found.

7. Among those working with Kane are E. T. Donaldson (B-text), and A. G. Mitchell and E. G. Russell (C-text). An important article on the text was published by Donaldson, "MSS R and F in the B-Tradition of *Piers Plowman*," *Transactions of the Connecticut Acadamy of Arts and Sciences*, XXXIX (1955), 177-212. Some of Donaldson's conclusions should not go unchallenged, but this is the most intimate and informative study we have of the incredible problems besetting the heroic editors of the B text. It is my understanding that increased administrative demands have drawn Mitchell away from his textual work, though he has added a valuable literary essay in his Chambers Memorial Lecture, *Lady Meed and the Art of Piers Plowman* (London, 1956). A more recent textual study comes from G. H. Russell, in collaboration with Venetia Nathan, "A *Piers Plowman* Manuscript in the Huntington Library," *HLQ*, XXVI (1963), 119-130, containing a discussion of HM 114, formerly Phillipps MS. 8252, which R. W. Chambers had examined earlier (reported in *Huntington Library Bulletin*, No. 8, October, 1935).

8. George Kane, ed., *Piers Plowman, The A Version*, (London, 1960). Morton Bloomfield reports that the recent discovery of another B manuscript has delayed the appearance of the new B-text. This manuscript, while not especially significant, is apparently deemed of sufficient value to require insertion of its readings in the corpus of variants.

9. E. T. Donaldson, *Piers Plowman: The C-Text and Its Poet* (New Haven, 1949).

10. Under the heading of post-war pioneers, I am including Bloomfield, Donaldson, Dunning, Huppé, Hussey, Kane, Mitchell, and Russell. In this connection let me mention two books containing important discussions of *Piers Plowman* that should not be overlooked. One is Kane's *Middle English Literature* (London, 1951); the other is Bloomfield's *The Seven Deadly Sins* (Michigan State College Press, 1952). A very valuable (but unpublished) work is S. S. Hussey, *Eighty Years of Piers Plowman Scholarship: A Study of Critical Methods*, M.A. Thesis, University of London, 1952. Published articles by Hussey include "Langland, Hilton, and the Three Lives," *RES*, n. s. VII (1956), 132-150, and "Langland's Reading of Alliterative Poetry," *MLR*, LX (1965), 163-170. It is impossible in my limited space to refer to all of the excellent studies written by scholars with other interests or specialties who, fortunately, paused long enough to do one or two articles on *Piers Plowman*. The following are examples of this type of contribution which I have found particularly helpful: Howard Meroney, "The Life and Death of Long Wille," *ELH*, XVII (1950), 1-35; R. Quirk, "Langland's Use of Kind Wit and Inwit," *JEGP*, LII (1953), 182-188; the same, "Vis Imaginativa," *JEGP*, LIII (1954), 81-83; Elizabeth Suddaby, "The Poem *Piers Plowman*," *JEGP*, LIV (1955), 91-103; A. C. Hamilton, "Spenser and Langland," *SP*, LV (1958), 533-548; R. H. Bowers, "*Piers Plowman* and the Literary Historians," *CE*, XXI (1959), 1-4; and Henry Allen Moe, "The Power of Poetic Vision," *PMLA*, LXXIV (1959),

37-41. In this category I would also include the article by Stella Maguire already mentioned (note 4 above).

11. J. A. Burrow, "The Audience of *Piers Plowman*," *Anglia*, LXXV (1957), 373-384. Burrow's point is that *Piers* differs sharply from the other poems of the revival in the economy of its use of alliterative poetic diction. Furthermore, "where we do find 'characteristically alliterative' words used in *Piers Plowman*, it is in a new way — for secondary, ironical effects" (p. 381). The examples given (A 3.9-14; 11.35; prol. 7-10) provide striking support for this observation.

12. R. E. Kaske, "The Use of Simple Figures of Speech in *Piers Plowman* B: A Study in the Figurative Expression of Ideas and Opinions," *SP*, XLVIII (1951), 571-600; "A Note on 'Bras' in *Piers Plowman*, A III, 189; B III, 195," *PQ*, XXXI (1952), 427-430; "*Gigas* the Giant in *Piers Plowman*," *JEGP*, LVI (1957), 177-185; "Langland and the *Paradisus Claustralis*," *MLN*, LXXII (1957), 481-483; "Langland's Walnut-Simile," *JEGP*, LVIII (1959), 650-654; "The Speech of 'Book' in *Piers Plowman*," *Anglia*, LXXVII (1959), 117-144; and "'Ex vi transicionis' and Its Passage in *Piers Plowman*," *JEGP*, LXII (1963), 32-60. A response to Kaske's article on the speech of Book was provided by Richard L. Hoffman, "The Burning of 'Boke' in *Piers Plowman*," *MLQ*, XXV (1964), 57-65. Kaske and Donaldson debate the merits of the exegetical school in *Critical Approaches to Medieval Literature*, Selected Papers from the English Institute, 1958-59, ed. Dorothy Bethurum (New York, 1960).

13. John Lawlor, "*Piers Plowman*: The Pardon Reconsidered," *MLR*, XLV (1950), 449-458; "The Imaginative Unity of *Piers Plowman*," *RES*, n. s. VIII (1957), 113-125; *Piers Plowman: An Essay in Criticism* (London, 1962). Elizabeth Salter (formerly Zeeman)), "*Piers Plowman* and the Pilgrimage to Truth," *Essays and Studies*, XI (1958), 1-16; *Piers Plowman: An Introduction*

(Cambridge, Mass., 1962); *"Piers Plowman* and *The Simonie,"* *Archiv*, CCIII (1966), 241-254. Mrs. Salter is also editor, with Derek Pearsall, of selections from the C-text of *Piers Plowman* (London, 1966), issued in paperback as one in a series of York Medieval Texts.

14. Coghill can be regarded as the chief pioneer and most famous advocate of *Piers* as a work of art, nor did his contributions cease with the immediate postwar lecture on the pardon already referred to (note 5 above). Mention should be made of his essay, "God's Wenches and the Light that Spoke (Some Notes on Langland's Kind of Poetry)," in *English and Medieval Studies Presented to J. R. R. Tolkien on the Occasion of His Seventieth Birthday*, ed. Norman Davis and C. L. Wrenn (London, 1962), pp. 200-218, and his more recent book, *Langland: Piers Plowman*, Writers and Their Work, No. 174 (London, 1964).

15. See my remarks in *Piers the Plowman: Literary Relations of the A and B Texts*, pp. 185 f. Further discussion of this issue is provided by George Kane, "The Autobiographical Fallacy in Chaucer and Langland Studies," *The Chambers Memorial Lecture* (London, 1965).

16. Henry W. Wells, "The Construction of *Piers Plowman,"* *PMLA*, XLIV (1929), 123-140; Nevill K. Coghill, "The Character of *Piers Plowman* Considered from the B-Text," *MÆ*, II (1933), 108-135; and a second article by Wells, "The Philosophy of *Piers Plowman,"* *PMLA*, LIII (1938), 339-349. As Frank points out (*Piers Plowman and the Scheme of Salvation*, p. 7), R. W. Chambers gave his authoritative support to the Wells-Coghill conception in *Man's Unconquerable Mind* (London, 1939), pp. 88-171.

17. This is the moment to mention Frank's important article, "The Art of Reading Medieval Personification Allegory," *ELH*, XX (1953), 237-250. I certainly agree with Frank's definition of

the nature of allegory as it applies to the A-text. But I do have reservations about its application to the B-text (e.g., B XVI, 1-89), where it seems to me Robertson and Huppé provide a valuable corrective.

18. Another book appeared the following year: Hans Bruneder, *Personifikation und Symbol in William Langlands Piers Plowman* (Wien, 1963).

19. See note 1 above.

20. See Morton W. Bloomfield, "Symbolism in Medieval Literature," *MP*, LVI (1958), 73-81. Robertson has made no reply to this, but his differences with Bloomfield can be detected from time to time in *A Preface to Chaucer* (Princeton, 1962) by anyone reading with an awareness of the argument.

21. John F. Adams, "*Piers Plowman* and the Three Ages of Man," *JEGP*, LXI (1962), 23-41; Ben H. Smith, *Traditional Imagery of Charity in Piers Plowman* (The Hague, 1966); Edward Vasta, "Truth, the Best Treasure, in *Piers Plowman*," *PQ*, XLIV (1965), 17-29; and the same, *The Spiritual Basis of Piers Plowman* (The Hague, 1965).

22. P. M. Kean, a review of George Kane's edition of *Piers Plowman*, *Library*, XVI (1961), 218-224; the same, "Love, Law, and *Lewte* in *Piers Plowman*," *RES*, n. s. XV (1964), 241-261; the same, "Langland on the Incarnation," *RES*, n.s. XVI (1965), 349-363.

23. A. C. Spearing, "The Development of a Theme in *Piers Plowman*," *RES*, n. s. XI (1960), 241-253; the same, "Verbal Repetition in *Piers Plowman* B and C," *JEGP*, LXII (1963), 722-737; the same, *Criticism and Medieval Poetry* (London, 1964). The valuable fourth chapter of Spearing's book, "The Art of Preaching and *Piers Plowman*," is handily reprinted in the paperback, *Chaucer and His Contemporaries: Essays on Medieval Literature*

and Thought, edited with introduction by Helaine Newstead (New York, 1968), pp. 255-282.

24. Rosemary Woolf, "Some Non-Medieval Qualities of *Piers Plowman*," *Essays in Criticism,* XII (1962), 111-125; John Burrow, "The Action of Langland's Second Vision," *Essays in Criticism,* XIV (1965), 247-268; Charles Muscatine, "Locus of Action in Medieval Narrative," *RPh,* XVII (1963), 115-122.

25. This is a central thesis of my book, *Piers the Plowman: Literary Relations of the A and B Texts,* beginning with the second chapter.

26. Burrow speaks of the B-text in his article, but the structure he is describing is actually that which was inherited from the A-text.

27. See note 24 above for reference to Muscatine's article.

28. Muscatine, p. 122.

29. V. H. Galbraith, "Thomas Walsingham and the Saint Albans Chronicle, 1272-1422," *English Historical Review,* XLVII (1932), 12-30. Examples of changes in the C-text would be the deletion of the earlier criticisms (in B) of bishops, and the addition of an extended critique on beggars.

30. Miss Newstead is to be commended for including in *Chaucer and His Contemporaries* (note 23 above) the translated extract from Froissart's *Chronicle* on the Peasants' Revolt of 1381. The book as a whole strikes a judicious balance between the traditional scholarship and literary criticism.

Sir Gawain and the
Green Knight

by Donald R. Howard

Early in 1961 Morton Bloomfield published an appraisal of *Sir Gawain and the Green Knight*[1] in which he urged that criticism had not yet come to grips with the poem. His sentiments must have reflected as well as stimulated a widespread feeling. Five years later Professor Zacher and I, starting an anthology of recent *Gawain* studies, found ourselves deluged with a steady stream of books and a flash flood of articles, from which we chose twenty-three items, the earliest dated 1959 and the latest 1966. If articles keep appearing at the same rate all such anthologies (there are now three)[2] will be obsolete by 1971; but they will at any rate have memorialized a burst of scholarly and critical activity whose suddenness cries out for explanation no less than the poem itself.

Imagine a student of *Sir Gawain* falling into a deep sleep in 1961 just when Bloomfield's article might have kept him on his feet, and waking up now at the close of 1968: would he not find a world wondrously changed? — the venerable Tolkien and Gordon edition revised;[3] a new Everyman edition by A. C. Cawley[4] intended for beginners; a computerized concordance of the four poems of Cotton Nero A.x plus *St. Erkenwald* (containing, it is said, some errors);[5] the entry in the new Wells (or Severs) *Manual* splendidly revised by Helaine Newstead;[6] four new translations;[7] three critical books plus a monograph; three anthologies of criticism; and, by a rough count, fifty articles. To be sure, many questions about readings, dialect, date, and authorship are still unsettled. The notion that one author wrote the four poems in the manuscript is still generally believed (though a few of us remain skeptics); that he also wrote *St. Erkenwald* was discredited in 1965 by Larry Benson.[8] As to criticism, my imagined sleeper would wake to a collective appraisal which makes the poem vastly more complicated — at once more comic and more serious, more arcanely religious and more secular, more structured and yet more variegated in style and meaning. It is a more difficult poem for all these critical possibilities, but he who woke after seven years would wake to find himself more in light than in darkness.

Have we yet come to grips with the poem? Though editorial and lexical efforts filter through from the philological underground, the dominant line has been interpretation. And interpretation, with an exception here and there, is notably historical: everyone wants to understand *Sir Gawain* as a medieval poem, a work typical of its age and of its background. Of course it *is* a medieval poem — even if the manuscript were found to be a nineteenth-century forgery it would have to be reckoned "medieval" in several important senses; but whether it is typical either of romance or of the fourteenth century is another question, and one that is rarely asked.

In Bloomfield's article of 1961 there were several kinds of studies which — in the curious parlance of academics — he "called for." This is often like calling spirits from the vasty deep: I do not find for example that anyone has taken up Bloomfield's suggestion of studying the literary function of verb tenses in the poem, the Arthurian and chivalric revivals of the fourteeenth century, or the surge then of English nationalism. But in other respects his hopes were fulfilled, sometimes in spades, and of these fulfilled hopes I shall make an inventory:

(1) *A study of the structure of the poem.* Bloomfield thought the structure might be based on the nine initial capitals of the manuscript, rather than the four larger ones, as is normally thought — a notion which I hopefully laid to rest in an article on the "structure and symmetry" of the poem,[9] though it was afterwards given some artifical respiration by Professor Tuttleson.[10]

(2) *A study of fourteenth-century attitudes toward style, especially high style, and toward rhetoric and poetic theory.* To my knowledge no one has taken this suggestion literally and studied the poem in detail against contemporary *theories* of style. But the style itself, and its background in tradition, have been studied in a very technical way by Marie Borroff.[11] To a large extent Miss Borroff's book concentrates on the tradition of alliterative verse and on the aspects of that tradition which gave some words a more elevated stylistic function than others. Her findings are useful in a practical way, since they indicate how the poet used the traditional diction; what we learn is a method and frame of reference for grasping the style of this poem. She raises interesting questions and it is exciting to watch a brilliant mind at work; but there are puzzles too — what for example does she *really* think about stress in

spoken English? Does she mean to ignore structural linguistics altogether and grant only that there is something more than the mere "weak and strong" stresses of traditional prosody? She seems skeptical that there are four grades of stress,[12] dubious that they play a role in poetic meter, tentative about a "tendency to isochrony." "Stress" does not appear in her index. She thinks the line "To me, fair friend, you never can be old" would have equal stress on "fair" and "friend" in spoken English, but more on "friend" in poetry (p. 192). The reader, in all this struggling with detail and pondering whether it is he or Miss Borroff who has the tin ear, will find that style and meter get somehow detached from one another. One longs for all the analytic shards to be pieced together, even just for one little demonstration passage. After fifty pages of learned foot-scraping and throat-clearing, there are forty pages of comment on Brink's studies; then a detailed — and splendid — chapter describing the style as reflected in the language-use of the narrator, with emphasis on diction. The last hundred or so pages are a technical study of the meter, an appendix as it actually is; Miss Borroff shares with her mentor Kökeritz a fondness for masses of evidence and few conclusions, so that he who asks what he has learned about the prosody of *Sir Gawain* will, leafing back, find some conclusions unsurprising: *-e* was sounded less often than in Chaucer, and does not count as a syllable in the long lines; whether it was sounded at the ends of lines is left an open question (p. 189). Her theory of the scansion (four major stresses per long line, and no "extended" lines) is based on a concept of "chief syllables" which in some ways anticipates the theory of Halle and Keyser.[13] But the relationship between meter and style is never more than hinted at, and one is left with many questions about both: did alliterative poetry have a single traditional style? is *Sir Gawain* typical of that style? is there no stylistic influence from, say, French or Latin poetry? or from learned poetical theories or rhetoric? what makes the style and meter of this romance superior to that of others? is there any relationship between the style and the structure or form?

Style is not merely the sum total of haphazard choices from all possible variants; a style is a *gestalt,* a set of values and a frame of reference which is grounded in behavior and culture, and which reflects a world-view. Miss Borroff might agree with this estimate of style, but her inclination is to deal with the scramble of choices rather than the informing whole. Another way of studying style[14] is to focus on basic discrete styles, to isolate "a style" which various works have in common and compare it with other such styles. This perhaps goes in the direction of a "structuralist" stylistics; it certainly does not preclude myopic attention to individual stylistic items, but it does try to find in those items a configuration and to discern its relationship with the cultural background and the poet's consciousness. When we pick up a book we *can* distinguish the style, say, of a sociologist from that of a humanist, of *The New Yorker* from *Time,* of Hemingway from Barth. And this reality of style, as we truly experience it, is after all what stylistics seeks to explore.

Fom this point of view, Larry Benson's[15] treatment of the style is, to me at least, the most satisfying. He shares with Miss Borroff the conviction that there is an old traditional alliterative style which was revived in the fourteenth century. But he explores what this style has in common with other styles, including Chaucer's; he shows what it shared with and drew from the "high style" of medieval rhetoric; and he shows in what ways it departs from the traditional alliterative style. He also shows how the syntax serves an analytic function — how it organizes experience and lends precision; and in the patterns of variation which syntax allows he uncovers an essential principle of narrative struc-

33

ture which gives form to the poem as a whole. He then relates this style to the meaning of the poem, and concludes that the subject of this romance is romance itself (p. 208). This conclusion has been widely misunderstood, or else widely understood except by me. The author is *not* merely falling in line with the current fashion for thinking every literary work is about itself — he does not once use the oleagenous phrase "self-conscious artistry"; he is talking about a style which calls forth a tradition and a tradition which calls forth a complex of cultural attitudes — in short, a style of life. But that style of life, Benson shows, is here depicted and its literary style employed by a poet whose subtlety and perspicacity go beyond all traditions and cultural values.

(3) *Attention to the Christian and moral elements of the poem.* Bloomfield allowed that the poem is "fairly and squarely Christian"; he added that the extent to which it is so leads into the critical question of the poet's primary intention, and I am not sure there is much more to be said on the subject than that. In 1961 appeared a monograph by Hans Schnyder[16] glossing *seriatim* every object in the poem (except the girdle) as exegetical symbols — the trees in the forest, for example, mean the Tree of Life. The problem posed by this kind of symbol-hunting has been endlessly discussed, and the discussion has grown tiresome. That there were such symbols in the Middle Ages no one denies; that they account for a medieval aesthetic is taken on faith by a coterie. An interpretation characteristic of this group — the Fruit-and-Chaff School, as it might be called — has been advanced by Bernard S. Levy,[17] and I will summarize it very briefly. The poem begins on the Feast of the Circumcision, and Circumcision in the Old Law prefigures baptism in the New; there remains for Christians a spiritual circumcision, the cutting away of man's sinful nature; and this spiritual circumcision "suggests a pattern which is clearly related to the journey theme" as

found in St. Augustine and Dante. The journey theme in turn suggests the Fall, pride vs. humility, and the need for man to imitate Christ. This brings us to Gawain. When we first see him he is sitting on a dais, which suggests "the potentiality toward pride to which the nobility is prone." When he offers to accept the challenge he displays *false* humility, i.e., pride; and the Christmas feast, suggesting Belshazzar's feast, also suggests pride. Gawain's adventure, then, is a spiritual pilgrimage. The Green Knight is the devil; life and death are *spiritual* life and death; Gawain is armed with "the virtues of Christian soldiership"; he moves north and "to the left," hence toward the realm of the devil; the temptation in the bedroom is "the Devil's hunt for Gawain's soul"; and so on. The author acknowledges as a troublesome factor Sir Gawain's great courtesy to the Green Knight, i.e., the devil; but "Gawain's refusal to remain is parallel to Christ's exhortation to the Devil after his final temptation: 'Get thee behind me, Satan!'" The result of Gawain's ordeal is "a spiritual circumcision which leaves him with a scar from the nick in the neck." All of this is paraded with the customary *pompes funèbres* of footnotes, long quotations in Latin, and so on; the upshot, as regards the poem's theme, is new found wisdom for Gawain and a reminder not to be proud.

Such a reading, if it is that, gives us an awesomely humorless poem in which the chivalric, knightly, and Arthurian elements are the chaff which the wind of scholarship driveth away. Such efforts have produced in Middle English studies a backlash atmosphere where any mention of Christian ideas in a medieval poem must be tiptoed into with disclaimers. If someone were to say now, as Bloomfield said in 1961, that the poem is "fairly and squarely Christian," his audience would be looking askance and coughing. The same goes for symbols — the shield, the girdle, and (as I think) the Green Castle[18] really do function in the poem as symbols, but not "exegetical" ones; yet to say so nowadays will fetch raised eyebrows.

There are, however, voices of sanity. In 1962, Richard Hamilton Green[19] published an admirable study of the poem as a quest for perfection. The idea of perfection in medieval thought is one whose centrality Bloomfield has also insisted upon; and Green's treatment, too well known to need summary, keeps this idea in focus without blurring the poem's chivalric values and its comic tone. The poem's background in Christian tradition has elsewhere thrown attention on medieval ideas about "pride of life" and controversies about grace and merit,[20] and on "covetousness" or "avarice."[21] The degree to which such Christian concepts are consistent with romance tradition has been subtly explored by M. Mills and more recently by Ronald Tamplin,[22] and by some of those I shall mention later who explore the poem's theme or the author's intention. The work deals after all with a moral choice, and the only model the Middle Ages had for dissecting a moral choice was based on moral theology and so grounded in Scripture. If the poet thought about this choice in the terms of suggestion, delectation, and consent, or any other process happening in the soul, the conception would have brought with it some overtones of the Fall and of Christ's temptations. Such overtones are understandably present in much medieval literature, but to isolate them as the principal melody makes medieval literature quaintly inaccessible and unilaterally Christian. The real problem for us, when we look back upon the great works of the Christian past, is to know whether the Christian content of those works looms larger for us than it did for their authors and contemporaries; and that is an exercise in the historical imagination which deserves more effort in the future.

(4) *Attention to the comic aspects of the poem.* This is, perhaps, the central issue. If the poem makes us laugh, what

does this laughter mean and how much does it discredit the grimly serious moral and theological content which some find there? The poem is fairly and squarely funny, and this must influence our estimate of its tone and ethos. But comedy and irony are delicate flowers — touch them and the bloom is gone. If a critic could but capture the luminous surface of this work, its form and tone, and recreate an authentic experience of them, might not the content and meaning render themselves up as *données*? The problem with any treatment of any comic element is just that it isolates an "element" for scrutiny and thus distorts the whole. As with all great comic works — *Don Quixote*, say, or "The Rape of the Lock" — there is something profoundly serious at the heart of *Sir Gawain*, and it is exactly this relationship of the comic and the serious which we need to grasp. Yet it violates the spirit of comedy to state its serious meaning in serious terms, as it violates the spirit of irony to say straight out what an ironic utterance "really means."

Bloomfield in his brief remarks saw the relation of humor to game, to tensions and oppositions, and to romance convention. The matter was picked up by R. H. Bowers,[23] who sensibly chastised three previous articles for their undue solemnity; in doing so he called attention away from high seriousness to the poem's value as a sophisticated entertainment, a fiction, a conventional but unusually successful romance which achieves the effect of high comedy and is itself full of good-natured laughter. The "play-element" in the poem was studied by Robert G. Cook,[24] who pointed to the presence everywhere of games and play, analyzing these against Huizinga's conception in *Homo Ludens;* play is both profound and childlike, both serious and fun, and Cook found play of this dimension in *Sir Gawain* at all levels — in its language and tone, in its conventions and customs, in its theatricality, and in the games its people really play. Theodore Silverstein has found the opening lines themselves playful when read with a shelf of analogues at one's elbow, and these lines set the tone of the whole.[25] Tone is the real problem in this matter of comic "elements"; we need to explain not *why* the poem is funny but *how* it is funny. And, to make it harder, tone is to be perceived as much in ourselves as in "the work."

* * *

Of the more philological efforts, let me pluck out one for dissection. Early in 1968 the Oxford Press brought out Norman Davis's revision of the Tolkien and Gordon edition, resplendent with new readings and emendations, new punctuations, and lots of *z*'s instead of yoghs. The revision is extremely conservative. The introduction, slightly expanded, still reflects an earlier generation's frenzy over analogues. The bibliography gives another whole page of analogues, a whole page of "texts quoted more than once in the notes," seven editions of *Pearl,* and so on, but only four books under the heading "criticism"; articles are banished from this select company, and Miss Borroff's sensitive stylistic study is lumped under "Language and Metre" alongside Kottler and Markman's concordance.

The revised edition is a compromise between a scholar's and a student's edition which does not succeed in being either and thus leaves a need for both. Scholars will find Davis's notes too personal and idiosyncratic, and will be curious to know whether, for example, he used infra-red photography.[26] Students will skip over his long discussions of readings and hunt for explications of difficult passages or discussions of tone and style, but they will find little of either. There is a lot of useful background about hunts, castles, shields, and the like; and decent enough attention to puzzling words and phrases. But passages glossed or discussed show more allegiance to the original edition than attention to the real problems students encounter in reading the text. For students I would be happy to see a book like Professor Baugh's admirable edition of Chaucer — with linguistic notes at the bottom of the page, and with apparatus intended to *teach* background matters; I would be ecstatic if it had also the virtues of Professor Donaldson's edition of Chaucer — spelling normalized at least to the extent of removing scribal idiosyncrasies, and interpretative notes which explicate the text and point up critical issues. For the scholar it would be good to have Davis's careful text and glossary, but with notes and apparatus appropriate to a variorum edition, or at least to a "standard" edition like Robinson's *Chaucer* or Klaeber's *Beowulf* — I mean notes and apparatus that report previous scholarship and criticism inclusively, for the specialist.

Professor Davis's edition is weakened by his contradictory poses of genteel amateurism and scientific objectivity. Davis states in his preface (p. v) that an edition is not the place to put forward another "interpretation" (inverted commas, like secret-service agents, accompany this sensitive word); but in his notes he hustles in some very personal reactions disguised as philological facts. For example, a whole page of notes is devoted to line 1237 ("ʒe ar welcum to my cors"); Davis wants very badly to have it mean "You are welcome to me" or "I am glad to have you here" and so contrives to ignore the possibility of a double entendre, the sexual undertone of the situation and indeed of the passage. You would never know from his notes that there is any irony or humor in the poem; or that there is any ambiguity about the temptations or Gawain's confession. Again, on line 802, which describes Bercilak's castle with the simile "pat pared out of papure purely hit semed," he compares *Purity* 1407-08, where paper cut-outs are placed over dishes at a feast. He does not mention the reference to this custom in Chaucer's *Parson's Tale* (X.444), though it is a far more significant comparison; and he does not acknowledge Professor Acker-man's discovery of the custom or profit from his discussion of it.[27] Instead, he adds "It is evidently the elaboration of the castle work-manship that the simile is meant to emphasize; there is no sugges-tion that it was insubstantial." I find this a difficult inference to draw about a comparison between a castle and a paper dish-cover; and it is surely "interpretation" once you take off its philological false whiskers.

Before leaving the matter of editions I might mention that J. J. Anderson's edition of *Patience* appeared in 1969 but that the venerable editions of *Purity* are hard to come by. A new photo-graphic facsimile of the manuscript is needed; the last was made in 1922, and although the manuscript has deteriorated a little since then, photographic equipment has notably improved. It would, by the way, be interesting to know what a competent art historian could tell is about the crude drawings in the manuscript, which do not portray such significant details as the challenging knight's green skin and hair, but which seem to have a delightful vivacity and drollery. While on this subject I might record my dream of a book of photographs, like the late Roger Sherman Loomis's *Chaucer's World* (Princeton), and my other dream of a film as good as Naomi Diamond's and Mary Kirby's "From Every Shire's End: The World of Chaucer's Pilgrims" (International Film Bureau). To pass briefly from the visual to the auditory, a good dramatic reading in Middle English was done by Professor Paul Piehler and a group of enthusiasts from Berkeley for radio broadcast in 1965 and is preserved on tape but not commercially available. Caedmon has a scene or two read by Marie Boroff and Jess Bessinger; but there is no phonograph record on which all of *Sir Gawain* is read, a strange oversight in an electronic age.

* * *

If one were to make a checklist of possible kinds of criticism and stack up *Gawain* studies against it, the results, I believe, would reveal an overriding sameness of approach. There are a few journeys into the Jungian or mythographic underworld,[28] Silverstein's world-weary meditations on *topoi*,[29] and perhaps in Benson's book an instance of genre criticism. There has never been, to my knowledge, a Freudian or a Marxist reading. For the rest, most treatments are rooted in historical research and seek to find the poem's meaning by applying to it an extrinsic knowledge of "the background"; or else, in a few cases, they spring from the great rooted blossomer of intrinsic analysis, the New Criticism.[30]

About the New Criticism, now that it is over thirty, I will say only that biographical curiosity about the author never interfered much with our understanding of *Sir Gawain*, and that *explication de texte*, in this instance, has encouraged the search for historical and linguistic facts. Lately there have been articles on subjects like physiognomy,[31] the girdle,[32] the Green Chapel,[33] the guide,[34] the topography of the poem;[35] and such matters, though they may look like trivia in bibliographies, deserve plenty of attention. The same goes for scrutiny of the poem's formal characteristics. Its form is almost always viewed as an aspect of tradition, even though there is nothing else like it in medieval literature; hence much about it remains a puzzle — what, for example, is the real function of the "bobs"[36] and why are they written out to the right in the manuscript rather than on separate lines as in editions?

When a colleague asked me how much had been done on the "anthropology" of the poem, I found myself mumbling something about Speirs' "green man"[37] — and then describing Speirs' unhappy fate under the ax of C. S. Lewis.[38] Recently Helaine Newstead has challenged Lewis's famous scolding with a counter-scolding, as did Roger Sherman Loomis just before his death.[39] Perhaps after all Lewis did not understand what Arthurian scholars do

41

with their Celtic backgrounds. I do not myself find it useful to know that Gawain was a sun-god in happier days, or Bercilak a green man, and I agree with Lewis that critics should not use such details as mascara to give the poem an air of mystery — it has plenty of mystery just as it is. But specific myths, legends, and rituals were a part of people's lives then as now, and we *do* need to know how much such matters colored their mental content, emotional attitudes, and stock responses;[40] still, we should be prepared for the possible answer "not as much as some have thought."

This is no less true of the poem's structure. We can talk all we want about symmetry or organic unity, yet we know these are not conceptions a fourteenth-century reader would have brought to the poem. No doubt, as Burrow thinks, he would have experienced its stately and ordered progression in a linear way.[41] But this linear experience is nothing like the loose episodic structure of many romances — it suggests a ritual or game with understood rules, turns, and moves.[42] The principal events — the beheading and the temptations — *are* games; the hunt was called "the game"; and courtly love was often so called. Romance itself was game-like — as Benson shows, an elaborate *Glasperlenspiel* of variations on established conventions. Perhaps the poem's basic structure is metaphoric, with the conception "game" ordering it as the conception "pilgrimage" or "Fortune's wheel" orders other poems; perhaps the poet even had a particular game in mind — he mentions "gomen" and "laykyng" over and over, and in three crucial lines he uses the word "chek," a term in chess then as now. I do not suppose I mean we are likely to find anything as clear-cut as the hand of Ombre concealed in "The Rape of the Lock." But the nature and meaning of game-playing in the fourteenth century (which has perhaps not changed much since) might furnish an important idea about the kind of structure we have here. The relation between the hunts and the indoor games has never adequately been explained; and we have been the losers in trying to decide what rule Gawain broke or indeed whether he won or lost. There is something remarkably proportionable and almost mathematical in the way it all works out; and I will turn in my chips on this matter by mentioning Professor Hieatt's study of numerical composition and number symbolism in the poem.[43]

Some of the unsolved questions about "the background" touch on the poem's relationship to the society of its time. What segment of society was it written for? How high a level of aristocracy was it meant to appeal to? Does it reflect rural and baronial interests, or nationalistic and monarchical ones? Does its language or meter reflect a specific level of social stratification? To what extent is it "clerical"? To what extent were its ideas of hospitality, game-playing, loyalty, courtesy and the like obsolescent in the later fourteenth century, at least in certain segments of the society? Is it especially characteristic of a certain locale? Does Gawain's youth have social significance?

The "theme" of *Sir Gawain* is what draws the attention of most critics, and most themes put forward are based on efforts to name Gawain's virtue or identify his fault. Lately Professor Ackerman has grouped interpretations in three categories — those which focus on courtesy (in its largest sense), those which focus on romance, and those which focus on parallels with the grail-quest.[44] All three emphasize the ethical side; but Bloomfield suggested, and Ackerman agrees, that the poem does not necessarily present us with "a good man who emerges somewhat stained or humbled from his encounter with the world of evil or of the supernatural." Bloomfield felt that the humor, suspense, and tone of the poem discouraged this somber kind of interpretation. But few have taken the suggestion seriously. Hills fastens upon "covetousness," Burrow on "truth," I on "pride of life," and others on themes less Christian but no less ethical — "mesure,"[45] for example, or "tact,"[46] or "courtesy."[47] Benson thinks the subject is romance itself, by which he means (or so I think) the entire complex of aristocratic and Christian values embodied in this essentially aristocratic genre. Burrow emphasizes the interconnectedness of virtues in medieval thought,[48] as I have stressed internal conflicts within their value system.[49] But while some of us thus permit the theme to mushroom, we can well afford to ask whether a medieval poem must *have* a central theme.[50] We need to know more clearly what the medievals took for granted about the nature of narrative, of character, of "theme" or literary meaning, of meaning itself, of wholeness or unity, of visual or auditory experience, of consciousness, of language, of binality or polarity, of matter, of the world. In short, we have to ask whether medieval men did not approach a romance with different expectations about literary meaning than the ones we have — even if ours are better.

* * *

I have spent all this time talking about "background" as though historicism were the only lens through which we can look at a literary work; and perhaps it is. No formalistic kind of analysis — no *explication de texte*, no search for "patterns" of imagery, for structure, tone, or authorial voice — can even come near this poem without an imposing amount of historical and philological equipment. Its language, apart from all else, throws up an almost insuperable barrier between its time and ours. But in so far as our object is to understand the work, and not merely to use it as a potsherd of the medieval mind, we must remember that the poem was not necessarily admired in its own time, not necessarily in tune with its contemporary background. Why did it fall into oblivion? Perhaps by mistake; or perhaps because its form and ideas seemed old-fashioned at the end of the fourteenth century; but perhaps also because its style and treatment did not suit the tastes of fourteenth- and fifteenth-century men, did not fulfill their literary and aesthetic expectations.[51] Perhaps it was too ironical for them, too encompassing and variegated, too skeptical; or, to say it differently, too humanistic and too modern. In short, perhaps the real secret of its historical meaning and being is best indicated by our own response to it.

Historically the work has no role in English literary tradition, was a discovery of the early nineteenth century and not really an acknowledged masterpiece until the twentieth century. Hence we must face, more than we do, the riddle of every masterpiece; why do we read *it* but not other works of its time, even works which were then thought masterpieces? With *Sir Gawain* we are faced too with the riddle of every "discovery." Why was it not found sooner? Why was it found when it was? How much, for example, do we know about the libraries which possessed this codex, including the earliest on record, that of Henry Savile of Bank? And how much do we know about its discoverer Sir Frederic Madden? Professor Ackerman is now studying Madden's correspondence and his 45-volume diary, and this research into the discovery of the poem holds great promise.[52] Consider our idea of a "discovery." If you find a gold nugget among pebbles, it is not really (after the romantic fashion) lying immanent in wait for its destined discoverer; you have to have an idea about its quality before you assign it any distinction among pebbles, and from this point of view you do not *discover* your nugget, you *invent* it. Hence we can say that men of the nineteenth century invented this poem: that is, they conceived the idea of what to look for among the shards of the Cottonian library. And we can say that we of the twentieth century invented it: that is, we conceived the idea of what to look for in the poem which gives it the stature we honor.

The recent burst of criticism is a final phase in this invention of a masterpiece. What has made *Sir Gawain* a part of our cultural life is its power to fulfill *our* literary expectations, to speak to us as so many works of its time do not. This "modernity," or at any rate this pertinency, is itself an historical phenomenon of stunning interest. If a poem is something more than a text, if it must be read in order fully to exist, if its readers and its reputation and tradition are a part of its being, then *Sir Gawain* belongs much more to us than to the medievals — its appeal to us is more significant historically than its tiny reception by them. We must then submit to a grave self-examination our responses to this poem, *not* to scrape away what is un-medieval, **Coleridgean,** or post-romantic in them, but to uncover what *in the poem* has had the power to create those responses. It is simply a fact that after almost six centuries we *do* feel ourselves in communion with this anonymous poet, this man, this mind; and the rich life he brings to us, which is the real "background" of the poem, is the Middle Ages he knew. It is a fact which makes us different from men of Milton's time, or Dr. Johnson's, or Wordsworth's: a fact about us, a fact about the history and destiny of the poem, a new fact about the Middle Ages — a cold, historical fact, which we experience there, *with lel letteres loken,* in the work itself.

Notes

1. Morton W. Bloomfield, "*SGGK*: An Appraisal," *PMLA*, LXXVI (1961), 7-19.

2. Donald R. Howard and Christian K. Zacher, eds., *Critical Studies of SGGK* (Notre Dame, Ind., 1968); Denton Fox, ed., *Twentieth Century Interpretations of SGGK* (Englewood Cliffs, N. J., 1968); Robert J. Blanch, ed., *Sir Gawain and Pearl: Critical Essays* (Bloomington, Ind., 1966).

3. Norman Davis, ed., *SGGK* (2nd edn., Oxford, 1968).

4. *Pearl and SGGK*, Everyman, No. 346 (London and New York, 1962).

5. Barnet Kottler and Alan M. Markman, *A Concordance to Five Middle English Poems* (Univ. of Pittsburgh, 1966).

6. J. Burke Severs, ed., *A Manual of the Writings in Middle English 1050-1500*, I, Romances (New Haven, 1967), pp. 54-57, 238-243.

7. John Gardner in *The Complete Works of the Gawain-Poet* (Chicago, 1965), pp. 223-324; James L. Rosenberg, *SGGK*, ed. James R. Kreuzer (New York, 1966); Marie Borroff, *SGGK: A New Verse Translation* (New York, 1967); and Margaret Williams in *The Pearl-Poet: His Complete Works* (New York, 1967). A comparative critical study of the merits of these recent translations, each very good in its way, would make a fine essay. To my knowledge they have only been reviewed separately.

8. "The Authorship of *St. Erkenwald*," *JEGP*, LXIV (1965), 393-405. See D. S. Brewer, "The Gawain-Poet: A General Appreciation of Four Poems," *Essays in Criticism*, XVII (1967), 130-142, who compares the poems in a literary way with a single author in mind.

9. "Structure and Symmetry in *Sir Gawain*," *Speculum*, XXXIX (1964), 425-433. For a further contribution to the problem of structure, see note 43 below.

10. James W. Tuttleson, "The Manuscript Divisions of *SGGK*," *Speculum*, XLI (1966), 304-310.

11. Marie Borroff, *SGGK: A Stylistic and Metrical Study*, Yale Studies in English, No. 152 (New Haven and London, 1962).

12. On p. 272, note 7, she refers to the four phonemic grades of stress "posited" by Block and Trager.

13. Morris Halle and Samuel Jay Keyser, "Chaucer and the Study of Prosody," *CE*, XXVIII (1966), 187-219.

14. *The Three Temptations: Medieval Man in Search of the World* (Princeton, 1966), pp. 241-254, 257-301.

15. Larry D. Benson, *Art and Tradition in SGGK* (New Brunswick, N. J., 1965), esp. pp. 110-166.

16. *SGGK: An Essay in Interpretation*, Cooper Monographs, No. 6 (Bern, 1961).

17. "Gawain's Spiritual Journey: *Imitatio Christi* in *SGGK*," *AnM*, VI (1965), 65-106. For a more moderate "patristic" commentary see Gardner, pp. 13-36.

18. Schnyder thinks the castle is the Heavenly City (pp. 55-56); Levy says only that "the illusive quality of the Devil's workmanship is apparent here" (p. 92); Mother Carson thinks it the Other World (see note 40 below); I argue in a forthcoming

article called "Renaissance World-Alienation" that it symbolizes the world.

19. "Gawain's Shield and the Quest for Perfection," *ELH*, XXIX (1962), 121-139.

20. *The Three Temptations*, esp. pp. 217-241, and Larry S. Champion, "Grace vs. Merit in *SGGK*," *MLQ*, XXVIII (1967), 413-425.

21. David Farley Hills, "Gawain's Fault in *SGGK*," *RES*, n. s. XIV (1963), 124-131. See the reply by John Burrow, *ibid.*, XV (1964), 56.

22. Mills, "Christian Significance and Romance Tradition in *SGGK*," *MLR*, LX (1965), 483-493, and Ronald Tamplin, "The Saints in *SGGK*," *Speculum*, XLIV (1969), 403-420. For a similar effort, with emphasis on the romance concept of *chevalerie celestial*, see G. V. Smithers, "What *SGGK* is About," *MÆ*, XXXII (1963), 171-189.

23. "*GGK* as Entertainment," *MLQ*, XXIV (1963), 333-341.

24. "The Play-Element in *SGGK*," *TSE*, XIII (1963), 5-31.

25. Theodore Silverstein, "*Sir Gawain*, Dear Brutus, and Britain's Fortunate Founding: A Study in Comedy and Convention," *MP*, LXII (1965), 189-206. In contrast to the way Silverstein by indirections finds directions out, Alfred David, in "Gawain and Aeneas," *ES*, XLIX (1968), 402-409, argues directly and persuasively that the "tulk" of line 3 is Aeneas and "trewest" in line 4 refers to him; that a true man can be treacherous, David observes, is consistent with the poet's ironic and compassionate view of Gawain. Another view of the comic aspects is that of Sacvan Bercovitch, "Romance and Anti-Romance in *SGGK*," *PQ*, XLIV (1965), 30-37. Still another, J. Saperstein, "Some Observations on *SGGK*," *ESA*, V (1962), 29-36.

26. The Assistant Keeper of Manuscripts at the British Museum kindly informs me that there is no record of ultra-violet or infra-red treatment of this manuscript. Illuminated manuscipts are not generally allowed to be submitted to these kinds of light at the British Museum, though one would think an exception might be made here for the sake of an accurate text; the illuminations and drawings are hardly the work of a master.

27. Robert W. Ackerman, " 'Pared out of Paper': *Gawain* 802 and *Purity* 1408," *JEGP*, LVI (1957), 410-417.

28. In Charles Moorman, *A Knyght There Was: The Evolution of the Knight in Literature* (Lexington, Ky., 1967), pp. 58-75, the quest is viewed as a *rite de passage* and the poem as one piece in the archetypal jigsaw of the Arthurian tragedy; the poem "ends in the hollow laughter of the doomed court." In Stephen Manning, "A Psychological Interpretation of *SGGK*," *Criticism*, VI (1964), 165-177, the poem is analyzed as a story about the ego's encounter with the shadow (at this level of response). Manning is the only psychological commentator who avoids the direct leap to a favored archetype and employs instead Jung's ideas about the dynamics of personality; he is also one of few who explains, rather than assumes, Jung's ideas as he goes along.

29. See note 25 above, and "The Art of *SGGK*," *UTQ*, XXXIII (1964), 258-278. The many mistakes in the footnotes, misquotations, and misprints in this article are corrected at least in part in the version reprinted by Howard and Zacher.

30. The most notable example of New Criticism in the '60's is A. C. Spearing, *Criticism and Medieval Poetry* (London, 1964), pp. 26-45. Another is Alain Renoir, "An Echo to the Sense: The Patterns of Sound in *SGGK*," *English Miscellany*, XIII (1962), 9-23. Another, Cecily Clark, "*SGGK*: Characterisation by Syntax," *Essays in Criticism*, XVI (1966), 361-374. David Mills, "An Analysis of the Temptation Scenes in *SGGK*," *JEGP*, LXVII (1968), 612-630, is an explication.

31. Robert B. White, Jr., "A Note on the Green Knight's Red Eyes," *ELN*, II (1965), 250-252, shows that the red eyes means strength, courage, and virility. George B. Pace, "Physiognomy and *SGGK*," *ELN*, IV (1967), 161-165, shows that Morgain's black brows (961) mean lechery.

32. Stoddard Malarkey and J. Barre Toelken, "Gawain and the Green Girdle," *JEGP*, LXIII (1964), 14-20; the article argues that line 2226 means "It [the ax] was no smaller by reason of that girdle that gleamed so brightly," and that the girdle was worn, contrary to the common opinion, in full sight.

33. Mother Angela Carson, "The Green Chapel: Its Meaning and Its Function," *SP*, LX (1963), 598-605, argues that *chapel* is a double entendre echoing the archaic meaning "a place of heavy blows and carnage," the ironic hint only coming clear to Gawain when he sees it.

34. Paul Delany, "The Role of the Guide in *SGGK*," *Neophil*, XLIX (1965), 250-255, marshalls evidence against the notion that the guide is the Green Knight in disguise, and describes his function.

35. In an article not yet published, "Gawain's Green Chapel and the Cave at Wetton Mill," R. E. Kaske has reaffirmed the identification of Mabel Day in the Gollancz edn., p. xx.

36. Benson, p. 116, thinks the bob "is often meaningless in itself."

37. John Speirs, "SGGK," *Scrutiny*, XVI (1949), 274-300, reprinted with revisions in *Medieval English Poetry: The Non-Chaucerian Tradition* (London, 1957), pp. 215-251.

38. "The Anthropological Approach," in *English and Medieval Studies Presented to J. R. R. Tolkien on the Occasion of His Seventieth Birthday*, ed. Norman Davis and C. L. Wrenn (London, 1962), pp. 219-230.

39. Helaine Newstead, "Recent Perspectives on Arthurian Litera-

ture," for *Mélanges Frappier*. Roger Sherman Loomis, "Literary History and Literary Criticism: A Critique of C. S. Lewis," *MLR*, LX (1965), 508-511. An intelligent appraisal of this debate is Francis Lee Utley, "Anglicanism and Anthropology: C. S. Lewis and John Speirs," *Southern Folklore Quarterly*, XXXI (1967), 1-11.

40. Mother Angela Carson, "Morgain La Fée as the Principle of Unity in *GGK*," *MLQ*, XXIII (1962), 3-16, argues persuasively for the importance of Morgain, basing her argument on "the general tradition of myth and folklore known to the author and his audience." Cf. Douglas M. Moon, "The Role of Morgain la Fée in *SGGK*," *NM*, LXVII (1966), 31-57, a rather labored development of the matter. On the presence of pagan and Christian ideas of magic in the poem, see T. McAlindon, "Magic, Fate, and Providence in Medieval Narrative and *SGGK*," *RES*, n.s. XVI (1965), 121-139. The whole matter of folklore background deserves a dispassionate theoretical treatment, as does the general problem of source and provenience. Cf. for example Larry D. Benson, "The Source of the Beheading Episode in *SGGK*," *MP*, LIX (1961), 1-12; in what sense is "source" meant here?

41. J. A. Burrow, *A Reading of SGGK* (New York, 1966), esp. pp. 1-4.

42. On the game element in the poem see *The Three Temptations*, pp. 243-244 and 284-285; and cf. note 24 above. John Leyerle has in preparation an article on this subject.

43. A. Kent Hieatt, "*Sir Gawain*: Pentangle, *Luf-Lace*, Numerical Structure," *Papers on Language and Literature*, IV (1968), 339-359.

44. Robert W. Ackerman, "*SGGK* and Its Interpreters," in *On Stage and Off: Eight Essays in English Literature*, ed. J. W. Ehrstine, J. R. Elwood, and R. C. McLean (Pullman, Wash., 1968), pp. 66-73.

45. Jan Solomon, "The Lesson of Sir Gawain," *PMASAL*, XLVIII (1963), 599-608.

46. Morton Donner, "Tact as a Criterion of Reality in *SGGK*," *Papers on English Language and Literature*, I (1965), 306-315.

47. J. F. Kiteley, "The *De Arte Honeste Amandi* of Andreas Capellanus and the Concept of Courtesy in *SGGK*," *Anglia*, LXXIX (1961), 7-16. For a similar view with emphasis on chivalric virtues and a notion of "heartless" laughter at the end, see Gordon M. Shedd, "Knight in Tarnished Armour: The Meaning of *SGGK*," *MLR*, LXII (1967), 3-13. But cf. Kiteley's "The Knight Who Cared for His Life," *Anglia*, LXXIX (1962), 131-137, which I like to think supports attention to "pride of life."

48. Burrow, esp. pp. 42-51. For a similar view, nicely put, see E. T. Donaldson in *The Norton Anthology of English Literature*, ed. M. H. Abrams (New York, 1962), I, 183-184.

49. *The Three Temptations*, esp. pp. 271-223.

50. The problem is associated with that of "unity" — a matter opened to discussion by Robert M. Jordan's perceptive study *Chaucer and the Shape of Creation: The Aesthetic Possibilities of Inorganic Structure* (Cambridge, Mass., 1967). To avoid the implications which the word *theme* carries — the suggestion of Coleridgean unity, the possible reference to music or rhetoric — I adopted in *The Three Temptations* the word "concern." If the *Gawain*-poet does, as several critics agree, hold up a whole ethos for ironic scrutiny, then his "theme" is a tangle of associated values. As a tool for analysing the poem perhaps any one of those values, arbitrarily chosen, is as good as any other, because any of them is bound to imply other terms in the value-system to which it belongs. If this is so, it would explain why a critic who thinks the poem is about courtesy, say, can write as apparently valid a treatment as can a critic who thinks it about truth, or pride, or tact, or romance itself.

51. The existence of a fifteenth-century adaptation rather bears this out; if the later poet found it necessary to adapt, he must have found something unpalatable in the original. The comparison, with this in mind, could make an interesting study.

52. For some preliminary remarks, see Robert W. Ackerman, "Sir Frederick Madden and the Study of Medieval Literature," in *Medieval Drama: A Collection of Festival Papers*, ed. William A. Selz (Univ. of So. Dakota, 1968), pp. 69-77.

Middle English Romances

by Lillian Herlands Hornstein

"Be not like the empiric ant which merely collects, nor like the cobweb-weaving theorists who do but spin webs from their own intestines; but imitate the bees which both collect and fashion."

Bacon, *Novum Organum,* Aphorisms, Book I, XCV*

The Middle English non-Arthurian romances survive in nearly one hundred and fifty manuscripts and are among the earliest publications of Caxton, Wynkyn de Worde, and the Scottish printers Chepman and Myllar. If these romances have been treated with remote indifference or by some disparaged as lacking the magic of great art, their popularity over centuries should make us chary of any wanton dismissal of the genre; and they have not been neglected by philologists, folklorists, historians. So much indeed has been said about them that the most significant publication in the past decade is the formidable bibliography which they have inspired — Severs' *The Romances,* the first volume of the

new *Manual of the Writings in Middle English*.[1] Yet, sensible and
and seductive as are the theories which this bibliography records
about why, where, and how the romance came into being and
flourished, the latitude of our speculation is circumscribed almost
exclusively by the internal evidence of the romances themselves.
We do not have many external facts. For a handful of Anglo-Norman romances, certain author-patron relationships were suggested
by Miss Legge.[2] But for the Middle English romances we have
little to supplement our conjectures but a few terminal dates
based on manuscripts and paleography.

We do not quite know, as a matter of fact, exactly what these
pieces are, or their proper literary designation; or by what methodology they are to be defined, delimited, or differentiated; or how
many there were; or exactly when they were originally composed,
or even the relative priorities of composition among them; or
where, why, for whom, for what audiences they were intended; or
their method of publication — who heard them and where,
whether they were chanted publicly or read to private groups, and
whether at one sitting or several; who remembered, preserved,
disseminated, and wrote them down; then, who later copied them,
or revised them; or how well and how widely known were different ones in different centuries, or why different versions are different; or what is the wider milieu in which they were produced,
their *Kulturgeschichte*, the traditions within which they existed;
or whether they make allusions to public events or to private
scandals, or the character of the men who composed them, or
whether these men were paid, or by whom — the "care and feed-
ing" of *romanciers*; or whether contemporary composers discussed
their art with one another; or where they found their written
sources and their popular inspirations; or what their attitudes
were toward the questions occupying men's minds, or even pre-
cisely what these questions were; or the literary traditions and

rhetorical principles which molded narrative details and characters, determined the structuring and styles, and the techniques of scene-building, dialogues and description, language, prosody, even spelling and pronunciation — in short, the critical guide lines and the pressures within which they operated and which are responsible for diction, dialect, imagery, and verse, and even the shift to prose; or whether they thought of episodes and sequences as related by cause or by purpose; or whether the composer-poet was also a minstrel-reciter-singer who was at all concerned for the lexical and metrical integrity of his text, or whether each performance irresponsibly, and as some would have it, subtly but inevitably, produced a new set of variables or "formulas" within a patterned frame, or whether there was even recognition of a pattern and a frame.

Now, when we consider this abyss of ignorance, — which students of romance would agree to call euphemistically *desiderata*, — it is remarkable that Burke Severs should have been able to spin some 330-odd double-printed pages of bibliography out of this aery non-knowledge, and to produce quite the best bibliography available for any literary field or for any separate genre. Professor Severs, whenever he thinks of this achievement, can, like Sir Thomas Brown,[3] regret only that he has two hands too few wherewith to embrace himself.

In the struggle for a methodology to bring into focus needs and the resources recorded in the Severs bibliography we may, in a somewhat simplistic fashion, accept major critical perspectives — social, formalist, psychological, archetypal — or conventional divisions into such discrete categories as: *Bibliography, Manuscripts, Authorship, Editions, Sources, Criticism, Literary History* and *Literary Relations, Mythico-Historico-Cultural Aspects, Linguistics* and *Structural Linguistics, Computer Techniques, Meaning and Poetic Intention*, and so on, although each element contributes to the total view and overlaps and interlocks with the others, like Gawain's pentangle:

> ...vmbellappez and loukez oper
> And ayquere hit is endelez
>> *Sir Gawain and the Green Knight,* lines 628-629

The Severs volume reassesses all 115 Middle English romances dated before 1500 (Arthurian as well as non-Arthurian), grouping them essentially as in its predecessor *Manual.* The scholarship similarly aims at completeness, but the presentation is new, under topical subdivisions (e.g., *Editions, Language, Literary Relations*); and under each subdivision items are listed chronologically. Individual entries are not uniformly annotated (as all important items perhaps should have been);[4] still a reader can quickly follow the pattern and reception of the ideas which have stimulated "God's plenty." Though there is no way to anticipate fresh insights which will set research in new directions, it is likely that here are embodied the materials from which a future history of the Middle English romance will be written; no such complete history yet exists.[5]

As a romance bibliography, Severs' preempts the field, overshadowing its competitors.[6] More general medieval bibliographies of the last decade merit mention where they have sections related to romances. For example, five chapters in Beryl Rowland's *Companion to Chaucer Studies*[7] give carefully selective bibliographies which, though centered around Chaucer, are also relevant for non-Chaucerian romance, notably those assembled by J. Burke Severs (Romances), D. S. Brewer (Fabliaux), Robert M. Jordan (Narrative), Beryl Rowland (Imagery), and Tauno F. Mustanoja (Prosody).

Another significant bibliographical contribution is Fisher's *The Medieval Literature of Western Europe*,[8] a critical, authoritative glimpse of the medieval scholarship of the major Western European literatures, consisting of eleven chapters, each by a specialist. Had this fine volume either a detailed table of contents or a detailed subject index, it would be even more useful. R. W. Ackerman in his chapter gives a running critique of studies of Middle English romance; similarly, C. A. Knudson and Jean Misrahi include sections on courtly love and on romance in medieval French; and W. T. H. Jackson discusses the romance and courtly literature in medieval German.

These French and German surveys discussing valuable background materials confirm the absence of *modern*, well-edited and well-indexed editions of French, German, and Latin medieval texts — works of literature and works of criticism[9] — which are basic to a study of the English romances. To take one example, the most famous *roman d'antiquité, Roman de Thèbes*, is available only in an 1890 *SATF* edition which was severely criticized. Nor are there current editions of those medieval French verse and prose texts which lie behind Caxton's translations;[10] and lacking is a detailed study of the Old French literature known to or written at the Burgundian and English courts. Further study should reveal who read these treatises, where they circulated, the impetus, *Zeitgeist*, under which they were composed, who the poets were and what they thought they were up to.

Other bibliographical tools, differently oriented, do make important, if only incidental, reference to the romances.[11] R. H. Robbins and John Cutler have edited a revised *Supplement*[12] to C. F. Brown and R. H. Robbins, *The Index of Middle English Verse, 1943*. The romance references in Stith Thompson's six-volume *Motif-Index of Folk Literature*[13] have now been corrected, expanded, and brought together in Gerald Bordman's *Motif-Index of the English Metrical Romances.*[14] Study of this volume should be supplemented with an essay on "Folklore, Myth, and Ritual," by F. L. Utley,[15] who takes pains to distinguish between "oral" and "literary," and to caution against an imprecise use of the term "folklore source" for any medieval literary document. His prescient warning assumes major significance now that A. C. Baugh[16] has postulated that the romances were produced by literate poets consciously *writing* for *oral* presentation (by minstrels or public readers.) In the light of the Utley and Baugh analyses it is difficult to decide how to interpret or develop most meaningfully the data of the Bordman volume for further investigation into the romances. One obvious possibility, though fraught with the danger that comprehension of the romances may be retarded rather than quickened thereby, suggests itself: the recurring motifs and patterns of episodes and structures, heretofore considered folklore themes, could be realigned and restructured in the light of Frye's concepts of archetypal or recurring myths.[17]

Studies of the language, grammar, syntax, and dialect of romances are noted in Severs' *Manual* in appropriate general and individual sections; but we still do not have a grammar of the romances *per se*,[18] nor a study of the syntactical distinctions in different manuscripts of the same romance. Tauno F. Mustanoja's *A Middle English Syntax*[19] does cite romances, but only occasionally, as illustrative examples; an additional thirty pages of general bibliography and selective bibliographies which follow each section and chapter, though not specifically geared to the romances, refer to special language problems which they pose.

A definitive study of the dialects of all the romances is still a desideratum which by definition must await a comprehensive study of all the Middle English dialects. The Moore-Meech-Whitehall analysis,[20] long the accepted standard, has come under vigorous attack by Angus MacIntosh,[21] who condemns its too broad timespan, inadequate number of dialect criteria, "crude" handling of the evidence which equates graphemics with phonemics, and insufficiently localized sources. A full-length volume by MacIntosh, promised but not yet published, is eagerly awaited.

The importance of dialect for a full understanding of the romance genre was made patent in a series of articles by A. McI. Trounce, who argued for the tail-rhyme romances as a separate East Anglian-East Midland style.[22] Significant as was this approach in directing critical interest from content to form, his own criteria of prosody, vocabulary, and phrasing have been challenged in a continuing dialogue.[23] These disagreements re-emphasize anew the necessity in Middle English studies for firm philological foundations.

With the hoped-for completion of that major reference tool, *The Middle English Dictionary,*[24] it will be possible to undertake for the romances new kinds of word studies and word comparisons — the use of word-pairs and doublets, a rhyme-index, perhaps an index of puns and word-play.[25] We can also expect lexicography to be enriched with the history of ideas — a vital expansion of our horizons by the study of a word within a general history of thought, what was called by Professor Spitzer "historical semantics" and by C. S. Lewis "teasing out" various senses and uses. The few studies which have already been published show how very much the connotative ambience clarifies the semantic and aesthetic tension.[26]

Similarly, the usefulness of studies of names and place-names[27] in Lawman's *Brut* and in other Arthuriana, and of Magoun's *Chaucer Gazeteer,* suggests that, were parallel, complementary investigations initiated for non-Arthurian romance, they would illumine the text, as they did in Mabel Van Duzee's *A Romance of Friendship: "Eger and Grime."*[28]

There is now available the long-needed index of *Dissertations in English and American Literature: Theses Accepted by American, British, and German Universities, 1865-1964,* ed. by L. F. McNamee.[29] The volume would be more serviceable for a student of the romances had dissertations from France, Canada, and Australia also been surveyed, had those in comparative literature been included, had *DA* references been supplied, and had some clarifying annotations (e.g., "edition") been provided for titles non-descriptive or ambiguous.

Since a work of art is never altogether free of external circumstances and the romances at some point involve every social stratum in the population, the relevance of historical understanding need not be labored; varied aspects of medieval culture should be explored.[30] Without further independent resources, we cannot even tell whether the romances bear the stamp of their social origin, whether (to paraphrase a remark of Harry Levin) they were affected by social causes or caused social effects — culture-ridden or culture-forming (witness the distended debate on the origins of courtly love). The wider complexities of available and projected bibliographies are discussed by the Rev. Harold B. Gardner, C.S.B., in "Current Trends in Medieval Bibliography"; listed are 321 bibliographic resources in medieval studies.[31]

The materials noted in the bibliographies we have been reviewing encompass the full spectrum — manuscripts, editions, sources, literary relations. The past decade has witnessed "pastedown" recoveries[32] and manuscript "reappearances,"[33] of which the most dramatic is the reappearance, almost simultaneously, of two widely separated manuscripts of the *Titus-Vespasian Siege of Jerusalem* stories. The former, — the "longer" type of the couplet version (as Dr. Bühler describes it), — reported missing from the Coventry School library since the 1880's, has now reappeared in the Coventry City Record Office.[34] The manuscript supplies a unique collection of Chaucer's minor poems; and with them, in the second part of the manuscript, *Titus and Vespasian.* The other manuscript,[35] the "lost" Aldenham *Siege of Jerusalem,* which I was luckily able to trace to the Cleveland Public Library (its present location), is not, however, in couplets, as Brown-Robbins had supposed, but in prose. And surprisingly, its French analogue/source, discovered by Mrs. Phyllis Moe, is so close to the alliterative *Siege* as to sharpen considerably our understanding of the genesis of that poem.

Although the recovery of any "lost" manuscript is electrifying, the pressing problem of the moment is editions. Except for the nineteen complete romances in French and Hale[36] (supplied, however, with only minimal apparatus) and five current paperback editions[37] which unfortunately offer either normalized-modernized texts, brief selections, or outright translations, the past sixty years have produced only twenty editions[38] of whole romances with full scholarly apparatus. This means that some ninety romances are currently to be read only in editions prepared more than four-score years ago. Another need, in addition, is that every version be edited, or, in the alternative, that every variant from a basic manuscript be noted. To expedite the editions, a practical expedient would be to survey the publications of the *Altenglische Bibliothek*, Camden Society, *EETS*, the Maitland and Roxburghe Clubs, and *STS*, and thereupon to undertake a corpus of re-editions or republications with modern materials (e.g., dialectal, critical) supplied in introductions and notes. And even more essential before a tide of re-editing sets in, is a philosophy, a methodology, and specifications for editing of these texts.[39]

Similarly neglected have been significant manuscripts (which contain romances) — notable examples being the Auchinleck, the Vernon, the Thornton, Cambridge Ff.2.38, Cotton Caligula A.II, and Cotton Nero A.x. Not one has been individually edited as a unit.[40] Every manuscript in which romances are found should be subjected *qua manuscript* to paleographic, graphotactic, linguistic, and dialect analysis.[41]

> "The first qualification for judging any piece
> of workmanship from a corkscrew to a cathedral
> is to know what it is — what it is intended to
> do and how it is meant to be used."
> C. S. Lewis, *A Preface to "Paradise Lost,"* p. 1

Although the romances have never been considered difficult to understand, no one has been able to tell us exactly what they are.[42] Perhaps, therefore, the scores of investigations which they have generated should be understood as Study Materials and Work Papers toward a more sophisticated critique of the genre.

Critics of the non-Arthurian romances have remained surprisingly aloof from the dominant currents of contemporary criticism.[43] While the mainstream has moved toward close examination of the verbal components of individual texts, especially their diction and imagery,[44] comment on our romances has confined itself within the more traditional channels — linguistics, history, folklore, sources, analogues. Trounce, it is true, was concerned with verbal and rhetorical elements, but primarily as evidence for a dialect and "school" of localized poetry, not especially for their appropriateness in an immediate poetic context in a particular romance. The time is now at hand.

Another major stream of criticism — "the Scriptural-allegorical method/patristic exegesis" — has thus far also by-passed all but a few Arthurian romances. This method of examining a text minimizes close attention to verbal devices and to the texture of the poem, and instead relates semantic concepts to patterns of Christian thought.[45] The contribution of this school lies in its reminder of the pervasive omnipresence of a Christian culture (equated by these critics with "theological basis of life"), which often underlies symbols and imagery. But the "patristic aesthetic" has been sharply and I believe properly criticized for its failures in methodology and more specifically for its assumption that there was widespread assimilation of exegetical commentaries, for its forced application of exegetical interpretation to secular texts, for its patent misreading of and violence to the literal sense of texts. An explication and spirited defense of the method has been made most recently by A. Leigh DeNeef, "Robertson and the Critics."[46] The anti-Robertsonians, nevertheless, appear at present to offer the more persuasive arguments in this controversy.[47]

Similarly, the philological integrity of the non-Arthurian romances has not been affected by any dogmatic criticism which sought to trace their origin to "anthropological" rituals.[48]

Concentration on "subject matter" of the individual romances has usually described its *matière* in symbiotic relation to a body of lore, folklore, or myth, in which the Middle English poem functions as an analogue.[49] Other studies treat special problems, cultural and literary (e.g., "treason," "education").[50] While most critics have been content to acknowledge a religious-didactic stance as a *sens* of the English romances,[51] others have gone so far (I think occasionally too far) as to read into certain romances a morality or message which would convert the romance into a saint's life.[52] These discussions provide a necessary basis for our understanding, but by their very nature only a limited kind of illumination. They have not thus far helped fix that particular essence of the romance genre which gives it its unique character.

One response to this challenge of materiel may be called "impressionism" (stretching that technical term somewhat); wideranging critics find less significant comparisons of origins, sources, analogues than assessment and interpretation of the romances by

65

a totality of impression, the thrust which the genre exercised on its epigones. To Rosamund Tuve,[53] the medieval romance — with its quest structure, plot with "entrelacement," multiple actors and events given unity by the meaning of the events, "small but true human responses to very particular situations" — can best be understood by the impressions made on the Elizabethans and notably Spenser, whom it provided with the matrix from which he drew general ideas of plot structure, tone, and attitude. For Margaret Schlauch,[54] similarly, the realism and social detail of the romances and their fifteenth-century developments make them the true exemplars of the early novel. And most recently Professor Fowler[55] has argued with considerable effectiveness that the persisting emotional impressiveness of the romance never died; it re-emerged as the ballad.

Just as these scholars think in terms of the total impression which the totality of the romances made, other critics seek to release the romance from subject-matter categories altogether and, like the Cubists, to restructure the romance into its essential forms. The dichotomy between the "epic" and the "romance" as "epic gone bad," so brilliantly suggested by Ker,[56] is repudiated by modern critics. From Dorothy Everett[57] to Hill,[58] Gibbs,[59] and Finlayson,[60] they recognize that the romances have their own conventions and *modus operandi,* "a way of treating certain story-matter," inherent in their verse style and formal structure. Wehrli,[61] Mehl,[62] and Pearsall[63] similarly stress a "historical morphology of the romance," whose elements are "formal and literary conventions" — the "grammar" of romance. Pearsall's paper, the most ambitious and thorough of these recent studies, traces through some fifty romances the life-cycle of the genre by distinguishing successive traditions of medieval versification — couplet ("epic" romance), tail-rhyme ("lyric" romance), alliterative verse. Although each style deliberately absorbed a large percentage of the alliterative and formulaic, each nevertheless aimed at different effects. Yet, as Pearsall himself is at pains to admit, his divisions based on metrical differentiae break down under analysis: romances in alliterative verse are excluded altogether because intended for a courtly-baronial audience (his hypothesis, for which there is no external evidence). By this test is not the audience, rather than the poem, becoming the criterion for the genre, and is not the critic guilty of both the "affective" and the "intentional" fallacies? Other poems, clearly not romances, but composed in these same metrical forms (couplet and tail-rhyme), are not discussed. Nor does Pearsall explain satisfactorily how the metrical style — verse or phrasing — *functions* to identify the genre "romance" or, to take a specific instance, to differentiate the romance from the saint's life or fabliau. It ultimately becomes apparent that what is being analyzed is what the romance is saying (content/theme). Moreover, cautious disbelief is the inevitable response to a theory which by its announced criteria (e.g., four-stress couplet) should classify the *Squyr of Lowe Degre* as "epic" romance.

Dieter Mehl, in a like effort to analyze "structure," shows a similar involvement with "subject-matter" (e.g., fairy mistress, fabulous pseudobiography, realistic details). Urging that the word "romance" be abandoned, he proffers a term which he regards as more neutral and inclusive: *versnovelle.*

The oral-formulaic style[64] as a characteristic of the *non-Arthurian,* nonalliterative romances has been isolated and analyzed only by Professor Baugh,[65] and then only to discover something of authorship (and sources), presentation (publication), and dissemination. He has, however, in a series of studies distinguished by their mastery of the details and techniques of the whole corpus of the romances, made clear that "formulaic composition of verse in Middle English is by no means restricted to the Alliterative Tradition," that "oral" and "formulaic" are not synonymous, and that *lettered* poets could *write* for *oral* performance by adapting a "formulaic" style in which certain regularized phrases are followed by "predictable complements." Michael Curschman,[66] concluding from parallel evidence that it is not possible to make a methodologically valid distinction between oral and written composition on the basis of formulas, has argued that although individual formulas differ, *passsages* are formulas of *action,* basically fixed. In a structural design which includes a limited selection of standard motifs and set patterns of sequence (their most effective combination is said to be a *Brautwerbung* — the search of a hero for a bride), the linguistic formula is, so to speak, just one tactic. One could compare such tactics with the modules, standard components repeatedly used in a computer.

I may observe that long before oral formulas (a lexical-syntactic-metrical-morphological technique where stock phrases describe stereotyped motifs) became the stylish touchstone for critical appreciation of OE alliterative poetry, in these very words ("stock phrases," "stereotyped motifs") the rhymed romances were ridiculed and condemned. The insight given us by the formulaic theory supports Professor Renoir's conclusions that "concepts of imitation, influence, and originality have practically no value for the criticism of the oral-formulaic phase of medieval literature ... where we find constant repetition of the same metrical formulas, the same formulaic themes, and the same rhetorical devices."[67]

We are, in consequence, called upon to re-examine the whole corpus of the romances, if only to attend to the ways in which these traditional compositional elements are used, to the stylistic tensions they create when combined with other modes, and to the different kinds of style, tone, quality they achieve.

68

And another factor — outside the poems — may have to be considered. Perhaps as C. S. Lewis suggested, formulas were "as much a need of the audience as the poet-composer."[68]

Through a long historico-critical tradition, starting with Harry Bailey, students of the rhymed romances have been brainwashed into appraising the non-alliterative and non-Arthurian romance poets as "hacks mouthing their trite line-fillers before a noisy unsophisticated audience." But when we find these formulaic expressions used while at the same time a poet (like Hoccleve) is "consciously striving for a grandiose style through elaborate rhetorical devices and aureate diction," we must ask whether for the audience these traditional expressions did not in fact contribute to that ostentatious literary effect which was the poet's aim.[69]

Attempts to formulate a definition and thus isolate the genre "romance" by purely metrical, objective, non-denotional techniques have not succeeded. Having reached this stage, however, we may begin to explore Benson's suggestion that it is not so much the author's debt to sources, traditions, and formulas, but his deliberate departure from them, the unexpected innovation, which reveals "a new aesthetic."[70] Before the judgment can be rendered, romances should be examined for their idiosyncratic qualities — in what ways and at what point themes, characters, and episodes are introduced, how new scenes are manipulated, how these function with relation to theme and plot, how dialogue moves the events, who speaks, when, and how.

All critics apparently concur that even from such studies there will emerge only hazy borderlines where epic, saga, *chanson de geste*, romance, historical romance, *lai*, saint's life, pious legend, fabliau meet and blend. Arguing that a sharp division between "form" and "content" is artificial, Morton Bloomfield sees a distinction between epic and romance only in part in their differing structures. Where Vinaver, deriving his judgment from the French romances of Chrétien de Troyes and the Arthuriana, urges that the romance (in contrast to the epic) is causal and that events develop from the psychology of the characters,[71] for Bloomfield the *Gestalt* of the romance is its episodic quality, its seeming causelessness in the sequence of the narrative incidents. Where Vinaver denies what Ker believed, — that differences in subject matter can be explained by reference to the "the spirit of the age," — Bloomfield accepts Ker's distinction that the two forms (epic and romance) reflect "different eras of sensibility." When gods disagree what can mere mortals do?

The seeming formlessness of the romances may indeed be "a kind of conceptual distance between eye and object, which is quite different from the kind of control envisaged by the unities ... [So we may take the example of Tasso, who] compares the structure of his poem, specifically including its unhistorical infusion of celestial and infernal councils, prodigies, and incantations, with the structure of the world, 'which includes in its bosom so many and diverse things and yet is one, one in its form and essence, one in the knot with which its parts are joined and bound together in discordant concord.' "[72] The medieval romances, too, for all their mystery and imagination, fantastic feats, and wonderful adventures, exploit their episodic quality to mirror the nature of life itself, where characters and events, as Chaucer says, "by aventure, by sort, by cas," separate and cojoin, overlap and interlock.

Notes

*Paraphrase by G. O. Sayles, *The Medieval Foundations of England* (London, 1948; 2nd edn., 1966), p. vii.

1. J. Burke Severs, ed., *A Manual of the Writings in Middle English 1050-1500*, I, Romances (New Haven, 1967), based upon *A Manual of the Writings in Middle English 1050-1400* by John Edwin Wells (New Haven, 1916), and Supplements 1-9 (1919-1951). This paper surveys materials published since the Severs volume went to press.

2. M. Dominica Legge, *Anglo-Norman Literature and Its Background* (Oxford, 1963), Ch. vii, The "Ancestral Romances," pp. 139-175. She suggests that the pattern of society after the conquest led to the "invention of a type of romance ... which filled the place of a 'family' chronicle" and gave the Anglo-Normans transplanted to England some sense of association with the past of their new country. These romances deal with English characters and legends: *Guillaume d'Angleterre* (Titmarsh-Lovel families); *Estoire de Waldef* (produced in the Cluniac Priory of Thetford); *Boeve de Haumtone* ("cast in the form of a *chanson de geste*," possibly written for William de Albini, the newly created Earl of Sussex); Fergus ("written for Alan of Galloway, Constable of Scotland, perhaps to commemorate his marriage"); *Gui de Warewic* (composed by a canon of Oseney to flatter Thomas Earl of Warwick); Fouke Fitzwarin (composed for Fulk Fitzwarin V). Composition was inspired, Legge thinks, by such events as a restoration, a gaudy, a patron's anniversary, or the needs of one of the Orders; cf. M. D. Legge,

71

"The Influence of Patronage on Form in Medieval French Literature," in *Stil- und Formprobleme in der Literatur* (Heidelberg, 1959), pp. 136-141; cf. M. D. Legge, *Anglo-Norman in the Cloisters* (Edinburgh, 1950); cf. W. F. Schirmer and U. Broich, *Studien zum literarischen Patronat im England des 12 Jahrhundertz* (Cologne and Opladen, 1962) (crit., *YWES*, XLIII [1962], 77); R. C. Girvan, "The Medieval Poet and His Public," *English Studies Today*, ed. C. L. Wrenn and G. Bullough (Oxford Univ. Press, 1951), pp. 85-97; M. D. Stanger, "Literary Patronage at the Medieval Court of Flanders," *FS*, XI (1957), 214-229.

3. Sir Thomas Browne, *Religio Medici*, ed. F. L. Huntley (New York, 1966), p. 97 (Part II, § xiii).

4. Illustrative of a well-annotated bibliography is the W. F. McNeir-F. Provost, *Bibliography of Edmund Spenser 1937-1960*, Duquesne Studies, Philological Series, 3 (Pittsburgh, Pa., 1962) (crit. L. H. Hornstein, *MLR*, LIX [1964], 453-454.).

5. Since this paper was delivered (December, 1968), a volume has been published which partially fills the lacuna noted in the text: Dieter Mehl's *The Middle English Romances of the Thirteenth and Fourteenth Centuries* (New York, 1969) analyzes perceptively those complexities and ambiguities which make a sophisticated classification difficult. But his own division (e. g., "shorter," "longer," "homiletic") follows no critical principle ("shorter" and homiletic" are not congeneric terms). Cf. M. Schlauch, "English Short Fiction in the Fifteenth and Sixteenth Centuries," *SSF*, III (1966), 393-434. Compare the full-length studies for the Arthurian romances: J. D. Bruce, *The Evolution of Arthurian Romance*, 2 vols. (Göttingen and Baltimore, 1923; 2nd edn. 1928, bibliographical suppl. by A. Hilka; rptd. Gloucester, Mass., 1958); R. S. Loomis, ed., *Arthurian Literature in the Middle Ages* (Oxford, 1959); Loomis's *The Development of Arthurian Romance* (London, 1963; rptd. Harper Torchbook,

1964); see R. W. Ackerman, "English Rimed and Prose Romances," *ALMA*, pp. 480-519. Loomis argued for a "mythical [Celtic] origin behind many objects, people, and situations in [Arthurian] romance"—and in his later days was willing to accept a possible "ritual origin behind the mythical" (C. S. Lewis, *Studies in Medieval and Renaissance Literature* [Cambridge, 1966], p. 9). Laura Hibbard's magnificent *Mediaeval Romance in England* (New York, 1924) dealt with each poem as a separate entity, which she related to the others by the Index of Motifs. A. B. Taylor's *An Introduction to Mediaeval Romance* (London, 1930) does not advance the study beyond Hibbard and Wells's *Manual*. George Kane, *Middle English Literature: A Critical Study of the Romances, the Religious Lyrics, "Piers Plowman"* (London, 1951), in a revolutionary approach evaluated the appeal of the romances without considering manuscript characteristics, sources, genealogy, or chronology; but his study suffers in consequence from an absence of historical perspective and firm aesthetic criteria. W. T. H. Jackson, *The Literature of the Middle Ages* (New York, 1960), pp. 80-159, discusses the romances of Arthur, Alexander, Troy, and Thebes, but only in continental examples and contexts; English non-Arthurian romances are not even mentioned. Margaret Schlauch's *English Medieval Literature and Its Social Foundations* (Warszawa, 1956) considers some sixty romances, each given only a sentence or two for both objective facts and literary comment; her *Antecedents of the English Novel 1400-1600 (From Chaucer to Deloney)* (Warszawa, London, 1963), studies the romances for influence on and survivals in the novel (crit. G. R. Hibbard, *MLR*, LX [1965], 242-243; M. Lawlor, *JEGP*, LXII [1965], 297-303). In R. W. Ackerman's *Backgrounds to Medieval English Literature* (New York, 1966), the only mention of the romances occurs incidentally in the "Appendix: Critical Approaches." Baugh's chapters (note 6 below) remain the most compact, traditional-type survey.

6. A. C. Baugh's up-dated bibliography for "The Middle Ages," *A Literary History of England* (New York, 1948; 2nd edn., 1967), I, for text pp. 109 f.; Ch. viii (Arthurian), for text pp. 163-170; Chs. ix, x (The Romances), for text pp. 173-198. A useful series of Goldentree bibliographies (non-annotated), under the general editorship of O. B. Hardison, Jr. (New York: Appleton-Century Crofts) includes: A. C. Baugh, *Chaucer* (1968), see p. 77; Wm. Matthews, *Old and Middle English Literature* (1968), see pp. 51-62; H. B. Allen, *Linguistics and English Linguistics* (1966), see pp. 45-47 for items with passing illustrative references to the romances. See also *BBSIA*, annual bibliographies, annotated, and brief essays; and S. B. Greenfield's bibliography in D. M. Zesmer, *Guide to English Literature from Beowulf through Chaucer* (New York, 1961), pp. 332-336 (annotated). All the foregoing are available in paperback.

7. (Toronto, 1968), pp. 240-246; 262-267; 100-102, 119-122; 77-84.

8. John H. Fisher, ed., *The Medieval Literature of Western Europe, A Review of Research, Mainly 1930-1960* (New York, 1966), pp. 94-101; 150-152, 154-177; 199, 208, 210-226. More general comments, not specifically on the romances, appear in John H. Fisher, "The Progress of Research in Medieval English Literature in the United States of America," *English Studies Today*, IV, Edizioni di Storia e Letteratura (Rome, 1966), pp. 33-43.

9. There is no corpus of modern editions of *les arts poétiques* comparable to the texts used by both E. Faral in *Les arts poétiques du xiie et du xiiie siècle: recherches et documents sur la technique littéraire du moyen âge* (Paris 1924; rptd. 1958) and C. S. Baldwin, *Medieval Rhetoric and Poetic* (New York, 1928). Still unpublished is Professor Ernest Gallo's sensitive translation and study (diss. N.Y.U., 1965) of Geoffrey of Vinsauf's *Poetria Nova* (from Faral's text). See also D. Kelly, "The

Scope of the Treatment of Composition in the Twelfth- and Thirteenth-Century Arts of Poetry," *Speculum,* XLI (1966), 261-278; J. J. Murphy: "The Arts of Discourse, 1050-1400," *MS,* XXIII (1961), 194-205 (crit. *YWES,* XLIII [1962], 75); "John Gower's *Confessio Amantis* and the First Discussion of Rhetoric in the English Language," *PQ,* XLI (1962), 401-411; "A New Look at Chaucer and the Rhetoricians," *RES,* n. s. XV (1964), 1-20; "Rhetoric in Fourteenth-Century Oxford," *MÆ,* XXXIV (1965), 1-20; "A Fifteenth-Century Treatise on Prose Style," *NLB,* VI (1966), 205-210; "Literary Implications of Instruction in the Verbal Arts in Fourteenth-Century England," *Leeds Studies in English,* I (1967), 119-135.

10. These problems are raised in two N.Y.U. 1968 dissertations: H. Grinberg, *The Three Kings' Sons*; J. Stelboum, *Caxton's Blanchardyn and Eglantine.* A list of the French materials appears in B. Woledge and H. P. Clive, *Répertoire des plus anciens textes en prose françaises depuis 842 jusqu'aux premières années du xiiie siècle* (Geneva, 1964, Publications romanes et françaises 79); B. Woledge, *Bibliographie des romans et nouvelles en prose française antérieures à 1500* (Genève et Lille, 1954). See also C. C. Willard, "The Concept of True Nobility at the Burgundian Court," *Studies in the Renaissance,* XIV (1967), 33-48.

11. Reported in preparation is a supplement to the C. P. Farrar and A. P. Evans *Bibliography of English Translations from Medieval Sources* (New York, 1946).

12. (Lexington, Ky., 1965). The reference, at p. xxiii, to the "lost" Aldenham MS should be corrected; the manuscript is in *prose,* in the Cleveland Public Library, MS. W q091.92-C468, the John G. White Collection: Faciam[us] ho[m]i[n]em ad ymaginem n[ost]ram, ff. 77-99, ca. 1470.

13. (Bloomington, Ind., 1932-36); new and enlarged edn. (1955-58); see also Inger M. Boberg, *Motif-Index of Early Icelandic Literature,* Biblothexa Arnamagnaenna, VII (1966).

Middle English Scholarship

14. (Helsinki, 1963), Academia Scientiarum Fennica, FFC no. 190, LXXIX.

15. See *Critical Approaches to Medieval Literature*, ed. Dorothy Bethurum (New York, 1960), pp. 83-109, esp. pp. 102-104; Utley, "Arthurian Romance and International Folk Tale Method," *RPh*, XVII (1964), 596-607; R. M. Dorson, "Theories of Myth and the Folklorist," in *The Making of Myth*, ed. R. M. Ohmann, pp. 38-51; N. Frye, "New Directions from Old," also in *The Making of Myth*, pp. 66-83.

16. See note 65 below. H. M. and Nora K. Chadwick, *The Growth of Literature*, I (1932), pp. xiii, 5, and seriatim, arguing that widely dispersed people produce similar imaginative works under similar social and historical conditions, introduces another dimension to the comparative study of "themes" and folklore and "mythic" parallels. One may also ask what such parallels "prove" about the relationships of one romance to another. Critics who talk of "myths" or psychological "archetypes" probably see in these parallels the underlying, meaningful universality of literary works (Crane, *op. cit.*, note 47 below, I, 186).

17. N. Frye, *The Anatomy of Criticism* (Princeton, 1957, rptd. New York, 1966), espec. pp. 71-73, 95, 188-195; "The Archetypes of Literature," *KR*, XIII (1951), 92-110, rptd. in *Fables of Identity: Studies in Poetic Mythology* (New York, 1963), pp. 7-20. But see a necessary corrective by R. B. Gottfried, "Our New Poet: Archetypal Criticism and *The Faerie Queene*," *PMLA*, LXXXIII (1968), 1362-1377, and notes 42 and 48 below. R. M. Ohmann, ed., "The Making of Myth" (New York, 1962), collects ten informative explications of the method.

18. We do not even have a modern working bibliography of medieval linguistics.

19. *Part I: Parts of Speech, Mémoires de la Société Néophilologique de Helsinki*, XXIII (Helsinki, 1960).

76

20. Samuel Moore, S. B. Meech and H. Whitehall, "Middle English Dialect Characteristics and Dialect Boundaries," *Essays and Studies in English and Comparative Literature*, UMPLL, XIII (Ann Arbor, 1935), 1-60. G. Kristensson, *A Survey of Middle English Dialects 1290-1350: The Six Northern Counties and Lincolnshire*, Lund Studies in English, No. 35 (Lund, 1967), p. 246, summarizes the chief differences from Moore, Meech and Whitehall.

21. Angus McIntosh, "The Analysis of Written Middle English," *TPS*, 1956, pp. 26-55 (London, 1957); "The Textual Transmission of the Alliterative *Morte Arthure*" in *English and Medieval Studies Presented to J. R. R. Tolkien*, ed. N. Davis and C. L. Wrenn (London, 1962), pp. 231-240; "A New Approach to Middle English Dialectology," *ES*, XLIV (1963), 1-11. M. L. Samuels, "Some Applications of Middle English Dialectology," *ES*, XLIV (1963), 81-94, suggests the additional possibility of the existence of a "written literary standard." Of interest also is McIntosh, *Introduction to a Survey of Scottish Dialects* (Edinburgh, 1952; rptd. 1961). See also W. Nelson Francis, "Graphemic Analysis of Late Middle English Manuscripts," *Speculum*, XXXVII (1962), 32-47.

22. A. McI. Trounce, "The English Tail-Rhyme Romances," *MÆ*, I (1932), 87-108; II (1933), 34-57, 189-198; III (1934), 30-50; also *Athelston*, EETS 224 (1951). The dialect and provenance once established and the culture of the area reconstructed in depth, the romances can then be seen in a new way as local products, of local interest, presented to local people. Cf. R. H. Robbins, "The Findern Anthology," *PMLA*, LXIX (1954), 610.

23. D. Everett: *MÆ*, VII (1939), 29-49; *YWES*, XIII (1932), 94-96; *YWES*, XIV (1933), 118-121; G. Taylor, "Notes on *Athelston*," *Leeds Studies in English*, III (1934), 20-29; IV

77

(1935), 47-57. *YWES*, XVI (1935), 139. A. R. Dunlap, "The Vocabulary of the ME Romances in Tail-Rhyme Stanza," *Delaware Notes*, XIV, n.s. 36, no. 3, p. 33. Cf. G. V. Smithers, ed., *Kyng Alisaunder*, EETS ES, 227 (1952, rptd. 1961), 237 (1957), pp. 28, 40-58.

24. H. Kurath and S. M. Kuhn, *Middle English Dictionary* (Ann Arbor, Mich., 1952-) (1969, S. M. Kuhn and J. Rudy, eds., completed through the letter I-INV). See also *The Scottish National Dictionary*, ed. Wm. Grant and D. D. Murison, (Edinburgh, 1931-), completed through the letter N; *A Dictionary of the Older Scottish Tongue: from the Twelfth Century to the End of the Seventeenth*, ed. Sir Wm. Craigie and A. J. Aitken (Chicago, 1933-), completed through M-Mary; Joseph Wright, ed., *The English Dialect Dictionary and Grammar*, 6 vols. (Oxford, 1905); rptd. as *The English Dialect Dictionary* (New York, 1963).

25. Although investigation should be undertaken (since the romances are not without humor and *double entendres*), it is questionable whether the kind of word-play found, for example, in Chaucer is widespread or frequent in the romances. See Helge Kökeritz, "Rhetorical Word-Play in Chaucer," *PMLA*, LXIX (1954), 937-952; Paull F. Baum, "Chaucer's Puns," *PMLA*, LXXI (1956), 225-246; "Chaucer's Puns: A Supplementary List," *PMLA*, LXXIII (1958), 167-170.

26. C. S. Lewis, *Studies in Words* (Cambridge Univ. Press, 1960; 2nd edn. 1967); C. S. Lewis, *The Discarded Image, An Introduction to Medieval and Renaissance Literature* (Cambridge Univ. Press, 1964) (crit. A. D. Scaglione, *RPh*, XXII [1969], 327-329); Arieh Sachs, "Religious Despair in Medieval Literature and Art," *MS*, XXVI (1964), 231-256: *Accidia, Sloth*; W. R. J. Barron, "Luf-Daungere," *Medieval Miscellany Presented to E. Vinaver*, ed. F. Whitehead, A. H. Diverres, and F. E. Sutcliffe (Manchester, 1965), pp 1-18;

B. H. Hill, Jr., "The Grain and the Spirit in Mediaeval Anatomy," *Speculum*, XL (1965), 63-73: *Spiritus* and its relations to the "soul" (a "scientific" study); J. A. Burrow, *A Reading of "Sir Gawain and the Green Knight"* (London, 1965; New York, 1966): *Trawpe* (truth), implying a complex semantic range of moral and social qualities; D. S. Brewer, "Courtesy and the *Gawain*-poet," in *Patterns of Love and Courtesy: Essays in Memory of C. S. Lewis,* ed. John Lawlor (London, 1966), pp. 157-177: *Courtesy* as the opposite of indulgence in immediate selfish desire; W. O. Evans, " 'Cortayse' in Middle English", *MS*, XXIX (1967), 143-157: embodying such attributes as truth, generosity, politeness, hospitality, bravery, religion, the semantic range "by no means synonymous with courtly love"; D. S. Brewer, "Class Distinction in Chaucer," *Speculum*, XLIII (1968), 290-305: "degree," "gentil"; L. Gross, "The Meaning and Oral-Formulaic Use of *RIOT* in the Alliterative *Morte Arthure,*" *AnM*, IX (1968), 98-102; see also E. T. Donaldson, "Idiom of Popular Poetry in the *Miller's Tale,*" *English Institute Essays, 1950,* ed. A. S. Downer (New York, 1951), 116-140; rptd. in *Chaucer and His Contemporaries,* ed. H. Newstead (New York, 1968), pp 174-189: e.g., "fetys," "coy," "hende," "derne." Cf. D. H. Green, *The Carolingian Lord, Semantic Studies of Old High German: Balder, Frô, Truhtin, Hêrro* (Cambridge, 1961) (crit. F. Norman, *MÆ*, XXXVII [1968], 66-71).

27. R. Blenner-Hassett, "A Study of Place-Names in Lawman's *Brut,*" *Stanford University Publications, University Series, Lang. and Lit.,* IX (1951); R. W. Ackerman, "An Index of the Arthurian Names in Middle English," *Stanford University Publications, University Series, Lang. and Lit.,* X (1952); F. P. Magoun, Jr., *A Chaucer Gazetteer* (Chicago, 1961); cf. R. C. Stoker, *Geographical Lore in Middle English Metrical Romances,* Stanford University Abstracts of Diss. IV (1929), 43.

F. L. Utley, "The Linguistic Component of Onomastics," *Names,* XI (1963), 145-176.

28. (New York, 1963).

29. (New York and London, 1968).

30. Worthy of note are two useful anthologies of primary source material, both in paperback: *Historical Interpretation: The Sources of English Medieval History, 1066-1540,* ed. J. J. Bagely (Baltimore, 1965); and *Medieval England: As Viewed by Contemporaries,* ed. W. O. Hassall (New York, 1965) (original title: *They Saw It Happen,* Basil Blackwell, 1957). I think here also of other kinds of studies reflecting the history of ideas, for example, D. C. Allen, *Image and Meaning: Metaphoric Traditions in Renaissance Poetry* (Baltimore, 1959), pp. 99 ff.; M. Thiebaux, "The Mouth of the Boar as a Symbol in Medieval Literature," *RPh,* XXII (1969), 281-299, passing references to *Beowulf, Gawain and the Green Knight, Bevis of Hamtoun, The Avowing of Arthur, Sir Eglamour, Partonopeus, Knight's Tale.* See also historico-"picture-books" whose material is relevant background for the romances: G. M. Trevelyan's *Chaucer's England and the Early Tudors,* vol. I of *Illustrated English Social History* (1942; new impression New York, 1965); F. E. Halliday's *Chaucer and His World* (New York, 1968); M. Hussey's *Chaucer's World, A Pictorial Companion* (Cambridge Univ. Press, 1967); R. S. Loomis's *A Mirror of Chaucer's World* (Princeton, 1965). See also Henry H. Carter, *A Dictionary of Middle English Musical Terms,* ed. George B. Gerhard et al (Bloomington, Ind., 1961); Anselm Hughes, *Early Medieval Music,* up to 1300 (London, 1961 [OHM II]); Anselm Hughes, *Ars Nova and the Renaissance, 1300-1540* (London, 1960 [OHM III]); F. W. Sternfeld, *Aspects of Mediaeval and Renaissance Music: A Birthday Offering to Gustave Reese,* ed. Jan La Rue (New York, 1966).

31. *MS,* XXVII (1965), 309-321.

32. Neil Ker, *Fragments of Medieval Manuscripts Used as Paste-downs in Oxford Bindings* (Oxford, 1954); Ker's no. 919 (p. 87), MS. Merton College 23.b.6 ("Richard Lionheart in English Verse"), has now been more accurately identified as from Robert Mannyng's *Chronicle* by Professor Norman Davis, who has also discovered a "genuine" *Richard* fragment among the papers of the Duke of Beaufort ("Another Fragment of *Richard Coer de Lyon*," *N&Q* [1970]); L. H. Hornstein, "*King Robert of Sicily*: A New Manuscript," *PMLA*, LXXVIII (1963), 453-458.

33. Awaiting rediscovery are some three dozen "lost" verse manuscripts whose locations were once known (Robbins-Cutler, p. xxiii). It may well be that someone with serendipity will even chance upon new poems in a local library or in an open and public place; and awaiting publication are many prose manuscripts: see R. H. Robbins, "Mirth in Manuscripts," *E&S*, n. s. XXI (1968), 1-28. In Arthurian studies, the outstanding discovery of this half-century is without question the Winchester MS. of Malory's *Works* (*Le Morte Darthur*, ed. E. Vinaver, Oxford, 1947; 2nd edn., 1967). Vinaver's argument that Malory wrote seven separate romances has aroused and inspired a voluminous critical response. See esp. R. M. Lumiansky, ed., *Malory's Originality* (Baltimore, 1964) and the reviews in *BBSIA*; also C. Moorman, *A Knyght There Was* (Lexington, Ky., 1967); E. Olefsky, "Chronology, Factual Consistency, and the Problem of Unity in Malory," *JEGP*, LXVIII (1969), 57-73. The Lumiansky conclusion that the romances constitute "one hole book" is now supported in a definitive historical review by Larry D. Benson, "Sir Thomas Malory's *Le Morte Darthur*," in *Critical Approaches to Six Major English Works: "Beowulf" through "Paradise Lost*," ed. R. M. Lumiansky and Herschel Baker (Philadelphia, 1968), pp. 81-130. William Matthews in a new biography, *The Ill-framed Knight: A Skeptical Inquiry into the Identity of Sir Thomas Malory* (Berkeley and Los

Angeles, 1966) rejects as the author the Kittredge-Vinaver Malory of Newbold Revel and argues for a Thomas Malory of Hutton in Yorkshire. The renewed interest in Malory has turned critics to his sources, particularly the alliterative *Morte Arthure*; a group of extracts is edited by John Finlayson (Evanston, Ill., 1967) in the York Medieval Texts. William Matthews interprets the poem as a tragedy, dependent in part on the Alexander legend, in *The Tragedy of Arthur* (Berkeley and Los Angeles, 1960).

34. The manuscript is described by A. I. Doyle and G. B. Pace in an article titled, not unexpectedly, "A New Chaucer Manuscript," *PMLA*, LXXXIII (1968), 22-34.

35. See Phyllis Moe, "Cleveland Manuscript W q091.92-C468 and the Veronica Legend," *BNYPL*, LXX (1966), 459-470; "The French Source of the Alliterative *Siege of Jerusalem*," *MÆ*, XXXVIII (1969).

36. W. H. French and C. B. Hale, *Middle English Metrical Romances* (New York, 1930; reissued New York, 1964, 2 vols.): *Avowing of Arthur, Athelston, Chevelere Assigne, Cleges, Sir Degare, Eger and Grime, Emare, The Earl of Toulouse, Floris and Blancheflour, Gamelyn, Havelok, King Edward and the Shepherd, King Horn, Sir Launfal, Sir Orfeo, Sir Perceval of Galles, Robert of Sicily, The Squire of Low Degree, The Tournament of Tottenham.*

37. Branford B. Broughton, *Richard the Lion-Hearted* (New York, 1966); translated extracts: *Floris and Blanchflour, Amis and Amiloun, Richard the Lion-Hearted*; A. C. Gibbs, ed., *Middle English Romances* (Evanston, Ill., 1966) in the York Medieval Texts; extracts, with minimum of emendation, from the "best" text: *King Horn, Havelok, Floriz and Blanchfleur, Sir Orfeo, Amis and Amiloun, The Gest Hystoriale of the Destruction of Troy, Sir Thopas, Emare, Sir Degrevant*; T. C. Rumble, ed.,

The Breton Lays in Middle English (Detroit, 1965): *Sir Launfal, Sir Degaré, Lai le Freine, Emaré, The Erle of Tolous, Sir Gowther, King Orfew, The Franklin's Tale*; Donald S. Sands, ed., *Middle English Verse Romances* (New York, etc., 1966), complete texts, spelling regularized: *King Horn, Havelok, Athelston, Sir Orfeo, Sir Launfal, Lai le Fresne, Gamelyn, Squire of Low Degre, Floris and Blancheflour, Tournament of Tottenham, Wedding of Sir Gawain and Dame Ragnell, Sir Gawain and the Earl of Carlyle*; Robert D. Stevick, *Five Middle English Narratives* (Indianapolis, New York, 1967), normalized: *Sir Orfeo, The Cursed Dancers of Colbek* [from Robert Mannyng], [Gower's] *Apollonius of Tyre, Floris and Blancheflour, Ywan and Gawayn*. Cf. J. A. W. Bennett and G. W. Smithers, eds., *Early Middle English Verse and Prose* (Oxford, 1966); extracts: *Kyng Alisaunder, Floris and Blancheflour, Havelok* (crit. A. C. Baugh, *MÆ*, XXXVII [1968], 202-205.)

38. *Kyng Alisaunder*, ed. G. V. Smithers, EETS 227 (1952, rptd. 1961), 237 (1957); *Sir Amadace and the Avowing of Arthur: Two Romances from the Ireland MS* (*Anglistica* XV), ed. C. Brookhouse (Copenhagen, 1968); *Sir Eglamour of Artois,* ed. F. E. Richardson, EETS 256 (1965); *Lybeaus Deconus*, ed. M. Mills, EETS 261 (1969); *Floris and Blancheflur*, ed. F. C. De Vries (Utrecht, 1966); *Guy of Warwick*, ed. Wm. B. Todd (Austin and London, 1968); *Sir Launfal*, ed. A. J. Bliss, Nelson's Medieval and Renaissance Library (London, 1960), contains also *Sir Landevale*; see also the Rumble edition of the *lais*; *Sir Orfeo*, ed. A. J. Bliss (London 1954; 2nd edn., 1966); *Ywain and Gawain*, ed. A. B. Friedman and N. T. Harrington, EETS 254 (1964). Noted in Severs: *Amis and Amiloun; Apollonius; Athelston; Degare; Degrevant; Eger and Grime; Gawain and the Green Knight; Havelok; Sir Lanval; Lai le Freine; Layamon* (EETS 250, 1963), ll. 1-8020; *Sir Orfeo; Partonope of Blois, Sir Perceval, Richard Coeur de Lion; Seven Sages of Rome; The Siege of Troye.*

39. Despite the plea made nearly thirty years ago, there is not yet available a volume which announces guidelines or specifies caveats, or even alerts a would-be editor to the cruxes likely to confront him as he sets out to edit a Middle English romance. Varied suggestive items, though they do not deal specifically with the romances, are: MacEdward Leach, "Some Problems in Editing Middle English Manuscripts," in *English Institute Annual, 1939* (New York, 1940), pp. 130-151, and see p. xii; J. Burke Severs, "Quentin's Theory of Textual Criticism," *English Institute Annual, 1941* (New York, 1942) (rptd. New York, 1965), pp. 65-93; C. L. Wrenn, "The Value of Spelling as Evidence," *TPS*, 1945, pp. 14-39; S.R.T.O. d'Ardenne, "The Editing of Middle English Texts," *English Studies Today*, ed. C. L. Wrenn and G. Bullough (Oxford, 1951), pp. 74-84; N. Davis, "Scribal Variation in Late Fifteenth-Century English," *Mélanges de linguistique et de philologie: Fernand Mossé in Memoriam*, Centre National de la Recherche Scientifique (Paris, 1959), pp. 95-103; Fredson Bowers, *Textual and Literary Criticism: The Sandars Lectures in Bibliography 1957-58* (Cambridge, 1959); Fredson Bowers, *Bibliography and Textual Criticism: The Lyell Lectures*, Oxford, Trinity Term 1959 (Oxford, 1964); E. T. Donaldson, "The Psychology of Editors of Middle English Texts," *English Studies Today*, IV, Edizioni di Storia e Letteratura (Rome, 1966), pp. 45-62; D. V. Erdmann and E. G. Fogel, *Evidence for Authorship: Essays on Problems of Attribution* (Ithaca, N.Y., 1966), also includes an extensive annotated bibliography. A. Hudson, "Tradition and Innovation in Some Middle English Manuscripts," *RES*, n. s. XVII (1966), 359-372 (scribal practices in Robert of Gloucester's *Chronicle* mandate the need for more extensive study of written Middle English).

40. But see John C. McLaughlin, *A Graphemic-Phonemic Study of a Middle English Manuscript (Cotton Nero A.x)* (The Hague, 1963) (crit. E. V. K. Dobbie, *Lang*, XLI [1965], 151-154);

cf. M. Levison, *The Application of a Computing Machine to Linguistic Problems*, diss. Univ. of London (Birbeck), 1962; note 21 above, W. N. Francis. For Cotton Nero A.x, Professor Moorman reports that he has completed the editing of the texts and is now working on the glossary.

41. A few relevant items are noted in this paper. Some beginnings in this direction have been made by the published studies of Neil Ker, Karl Brunner, A. C. Baugh, Laura Hibbard Loomis, and R. H. Robbins. Mr. Ker has traced the history of the owners and locations of manuscripts, particularly those containing Old English; Brunner has compiled tables of manuscripts containing romances; Baugh has distinguished among the written source, the adapter, and the reciter. Loomis and Robbins each selected a separate vernacular manuscript and reasoned about the way it was actually composed and physically produced. Beyond the work of these few ground-breakers, almost no investigator has moved. See Karl Brunner, "Middle English Metrical Romances and Their Audience," *Studies in Medieval Literature in Honor of Professor Albert Croll Baugh*, ed. MacEdward Leach (Philadelphia, 1961), pp. 219-227; and Brunner's two earlier papers "Der Inhalt der mittelenglischen Handschriften und die Literaturgeschichte," *Anglia*, LXV (1941), 81-86; "Der Überlieferung der mittelenglischen Versromanzen," *Anglia*, LXXVI (1958), 64-73; cf. G. S. Ivy, *The Make-Up of Middle English Verse Manuscripts* (diss. London Univ., 1954).

42. For a philosophical discussion of many uncertainties of definition and genre similar to the problems which confront the reader of the medieval romances, see E. D. Hirsch, Jr., *Validity in Interpretation* (New Haven, 1967), pp. 148-150, and esp. Ch.iii, "The Concept of Genre" (crit. B. D. Korpan, *RPh*, XXII [1969], 300-313); R. S. Lucas, "Hegel und die Abstraktion, Ein Beitrag zur Problematik der modernen Kunst," *DVLG*, XXXVIII (1964), 361-387; for the implicit parallel problems

in differentiating the saint's legend, see Theodor Wolpers, *Die englischen Heiligenlegenden des Mittelalters, Buchreihe der Anglia* X (Tübingen, 1964), e.g., pp. 157-195, 253-258; 342-347; see below, note 51; see also Archer Taylor, "The Parallels Between Ballads and Tales," in *Festschrift zum 75 Geburtstag von Eric Seeman, Jahrbuch für Volksliedforschung,* IX, ed. R. W. Brednich (Berlin, 1964), pp. 104-115; for a suggestive comparison to saga criticism, see T. M. Andersson, *The Icelandic Family Saga: An Analytic Reading,* Harvard Studies in Comparative Literature, 28 (Cambridge, Mass., 1967), Preface and Ch. i, "The Structure of the Saga"; for a few striking parallels to the Gothic novel, see R. D. Hume, "Gothic Versus Romantic: A Revaluation of the Gothic Novel," *PMLA,* LXXXIV (1969), 282-290. Note also F. Lot, *Joseph Bédier, 1864-1938* (Paris, 1939): "The masterpiece is born in a pre-established framework and [it is] this framework that [is] under discussion." (Quoted by Andersson, p. 309). See also M. Wehrli, "Strukturprobleme des mittelalterlichen Romans," *Wirkendes Wort, Deutsches Sprachschaffen in Lehre und Leben,* X (1960), 334-345. Cf. H. Levin, *The Gates of Horn* (New York, 1963), pp. 39-50; cf. Frye's dicta (note 17 above, *Anatomy . . .*, p. 186): in every age "the romance is nearest of all literary forms to the wish-fulfilment dream" of the ruling social or intellectual class, though "there is a genuinely proletarian element in romance too"; "the grammar of the imagination" which the romance genre employs is "sequential adventures, in the nature of a procession."

43. See R. W. Ackerman, *Backgrounds to Medieval English Literature,* "Appendix: Critical Aproaches," pp. 127-142; cf. Arnold Williams, "Typology and the Cycle Plays: Some Criteria," *Speculum,* XLIII (1968), 677-684; H. Kozicki, "Critical Methods in the Literary Evaluation of *Sir Degaré."* *MLQ,* XXXIX (1968), 141-147; D. Daiches, *Critical Approaches to*

Literature (Englewood Cliffs, N. J., 1956; rptd. Norton College Paperback, 1965).

44. For the difficulties of the application of semantics, linguistics, and the "new linguistics" to criticism of the poetic line, see A. J. Greimas, *Semantique structurale: recherche de méthode* (Paris, 1966), and more pointedly S. B. Greenfield, "Grammar and Meaning in Poetry," *PMLA*, LXXXII (1967), 377-387. *Sir Orfeo*, a Breton *lai* (the tight-structured species of the romance genre) has, however, received frequent and astute critical atention. See e.g., *Sir Orfeo*, ed. A. J. Bliss (Oxford, 1954; 2nd ed., 1966); J. Burke Severs, "The Antecedents of Sir Orfeo," *Studies in Medieval Literature in Honor of Professor Albert Croll Baugh* (Philadelphia, 1961), pp. 187-207; K. K. Gros Louis, "The Significance of Sir Orfeo's Self-Exile," *RES*, n. s. XVIII (1967), 245-252. Bliss has also edited *Sir Launfal* and *Lanval* (London, 1960); see also B. K. Martin, "*Sir Launfal* and the Folktale," *MÆ*, XXXV (1966), 199-210. The long-felt need for a volume devoted exclusively to the Breton *lai* has been met by M. J. Donovan's comprehensive and analytical *The Breton Lay: A Guide to Varieties* (Notre Dame, Ind., 1969). Six French versions have been translated by P. Terry, *Lays of Courtly Love* (Garden City, N.Y. , 1963).

45. E.g., see B. F. Huppé and D. W. Robertson, Jr., *Fruyt and Chaf* (Princeton Univ. Press, 1963), p. 10: the poet's function is "to express in terms of the figurative and the fabled the doctrinal truth which the homilist and the confessor presented directly."

46. A. Leigh DeNeef, "Robertson and Critics," *Chaucer Review*, II (1968), 205-234; see also Henri de Lubac, *Exégèse médiévale, les quatres sens de l'écriture*, 2 vols. (Paris, 1959-64).

47. R. S. Crane, "On Hypotheses in 'Historical Criticism': Apropos of Certain Contemporary Medievalists," in *The Idea of the Humanities and Other Essays Critical and Historical*, (Chicago

and London, 1967), II, 236-260. Jean Misrahi, "Symbolism and Allegory in Arthurian Romance," *RPh*, XVII (1964), 555-569: "Of symbolism there is much in medieval romances, and it needs to be carefully and prudently studied, but of allegory there is very little, and that little is almost always apparent on the surface or else it is explicated in the text itself"; D. Bethurum, ed., *Critical Approaches to Medieval Literature* (New York, 1960); M. W. Bloomfield, "Symbolism in Medieval Literature," *MP*, LVI (1958), 73-81; J. F. Kermode, "Spenser and the Allegorists," *PBA*, XLVIII (1963), 261; F. L. Utley, "Robertsonianism Redivivus," *RPh*, XIX (1965), 250-260 (crit. *YWES*, XLVI [1965], 89). M. Bataillon, *Défense et illustration du sens littéral, The Presidential Address* (Leeds: MHRA, 1967); P. E. Beichner, "The Allegorical Interpretation of Medieval Literature," *PMLA*, LXXXII (1967), 33-38; R. Delasanta, "Christian Affirmation in *The Book of the Duchess*," *PMLA*, LXXXIV (1969), 245-251, esp. pp. 246-247.

48. J. Speirs: *Medieval English Poetry: The Non-Chaucerian Tradition* (London, 1957); "The Metrical Romances," pp. 34-39, in *The Pelican Guide to English Literature I: The Age of Chaucer,* ed. Boris Ford (Baltimore, 1954, rptd. 1966). C. S. Lewis: "The Anthropological Approach to Medieval Literature," in *English and Medieval Studies Presented to J. R. R. Tolkien,* ed. Norman Davis and C. L. Wrenn (London, 1962), pp. 219-230; "De audiendis poetis" in his *Studies in Medieval and Renaissance Literature* (Cambridge, 1966), pp. 1-17, esp. pp. 9 ff. (crit. J. Burrow, *EC*, XVII [1967], 89-95).

49. One is tempted to describe these analogues, in language borrowed from linguistics, as allomorphs, whose "rule" or "law" of "distribution" is not yet explained; cf. notes 15 and 17 above; see Morris Epstein, *Tales of Sendebar* (edition and translation of Bodl. MS. Heb. d.11 and Bodl. MS. Heb. or. 135 — the Hebrew versions of the *Seven Sages*) (Philadelphia,

1967); R. Reich, *Tales of Alexander the Macedonian: Two Medieval Hebrew Versions and Their Analogues in Middle English Literature* (Bodl. MS. Heb. d.11, ff. 265-279; MS. Modena LII, Estense Libr. Modena, Italy; translation, notes; diss. N.Y.U., 1967); Minoo Sassoonian, *The Persian Prose Version of the "Romance of Alexander"*: Translation and and Study of its Place in the Tradition of Alexander Romances and Its Relation to the English Versions (diss. N.Y.U., in progress).

50. O. Kratins, "Treason in the Middle English Metrical Romances," *PQ*, XLV (1966), 668-687; includes *Amis and Amiloun, Alisaunder, Athelston, Emare, Earl of Toulous, Florence, Generydes, Launfal.* An interesting study by Madeleine P. Cosman, *The Education of the Hero in Arthurian Romance* (Chapel Hill, N. C., 1966); includes *Apollonius, Alexander, Libeaus Desconus, Seven Sages.* R. Woolf, "The Theme of the Lover-Knight in Medieval English Literature," *RES*, n. s. XIII (1962), 1-16. H. Adolf, "The Concept of Original Sin as Reflected in Arthurian Romance," *Studies in Language and Literature in Honor of Margaret Schlauch*, ed. M. Brahmer, S. Helsztyski, and J. Krzyzanowski (Warsaw, 1966), pp 21-29 (incest the symbol of lust, and lust the symbol of Original Sin). J. F. Collas, "The Romantic Hero of the Twelfth Century," *Medieval Miscellany Presented to Eugene Vinaver*, ed. F. Whitehead, A. H. Diverres, and F. E. Sutcliffe (Manchester, 1965), pp. 80-96 (*lai* versus *romance*). See also, for example, the following dissertations: Wm. R. Barron, *The French Sources of Middle English Alliterative Romance*, St. Andrews (Scot), 1959; M. M. Lanham, *Chastity, A Study of Sexual Morality in the English Medieval Romances*, Vanderbilt, 1947; C. E. Long, *Shapeshifting and Associated Phenomena as Conventions of the Middle English Metrical Romances*, New Mexico, 1957; C. C. Revard, *The Medieval Growl, Some Aspects of Middle English Satire*, Yale, 1959; Z. J. Rouillard, *An Analysis*

of Some Patterns of Comparison in the Matter of England Romances, Colorado, 1959; W. W. Ryding, *Structural Patterns in Medieval Narrative*, Colorado, 1961.

51. I. P. McKeehan, *Some Relations between the Medieval Legends of British Saints and Medieval Romances* (diss. Univ. of Chicago, 1923). L. Braswell, "Sir Isumbras and the Legend of Saint Eustace," *MS*, XXVII (1965), 128-151, stresses the way one genre interacts upon the other, cross-borrowing episodes and sequences; see also M. Wehrli, "Roman und Legende im deutschen Hoch Mittelalter," *Worte und Werte, Bruno Mark-wardt zum 60 Geburtstag*, ed. G. Erdman and A. Eichstaedt (Berlin, 1961), pp. 428-443, esp. pp. 430-434 (parallels in theme, plot, and character). D. Klausner, *The Nature and Origins of Didacticism in Some Middle English Romances* (diss. Cambridge Univ., 1967). Dr. Doris Shores, ed., *The King of Tars* (diss. N.Y.U., 1969), argues that the initial conduct of the heroine is modeled on, or at least parallels, incidents in the life of St. Ursula. Apparently a king of Tars had acquired so great a reputation for piety that he became a fit protagonist against the Synagogue of Satan; see *Ovid moralisé*, ed. by C. de Boer, Verhandelingen der Kroninklijke Akademie van Wetenschappen te Amsterdam, 5 vols. (Amsterdam, 1915-38, rptd. Weisbaden, 1966-68), Bk. II, p. 24.

Quar, quant li filz Dieu vint en terre,
3446 Pour son pueple sauver et querre,
Onc reconnoistre ne le volt.

3448 Li roi de Tarse, o cuers devot,
Le vindrent de loing aorer,

3450 Par dons servir et honnorer,
Mes Signagogue, sa voisine,

3452 Qui par l'Escripture Devine
Sot ou dut estre sa nessance,

3454 Ne li fist nulle reverence,
Ains cuida murtrir, par envie,

3456　Le seignor de mort et de vie.

I am indebted to one of my students, Bernard Witlieb, for bringing this reference to my attention.

52. See O. Kratins, "The Middle English *Amis and Amiloun,* Chivalric Romance or Secular Hagiography?" *PMLA,* LXXXI (1966), 347-354: Kratins' arguments for "hagiography" are not convincing; cf. D. Pearsall, "The Development of Middle English Romance," *MS,* XXVII (1965), 109-112; D. Kramer, "Structural Artistry in *Amis and Amiloun,*" *AnM,* IX (1968), 103-122, esp. pp. 106, 114, 118.

53. R. Tuve, *Allegorical Imagery: Some Medieval Books and Their Posterity* (Princeton, 1966), Ch. v, "Romances," pp. 335 ff. Miss Tuve has generally been described as a "typological" "traditionalist" critic.

54. M. Schlauch, *Antecedents of the English Novel 1400-1600 (from Chaucer to Deloney)* (London, 1963).

55. D. C. Fowler, *A Literary History of the Popular Ballad* (Durham, N. C., 1968), esp. p. 182; contrast B. A. Rosenberg, "The Morphology of the Middle English Metrical Romance," *Journal of Popular Culture,* I (1967-68), 63-77, arguing that "most, and possibly all, of the romances came from folktales or ballads."

56. W. P. Ker, *Epic and Romance, Essays on Medieval Literature* (London, 1897; 2nd edn. London, 1908; rptd. New York, 1957). This pioneer study has never been superseded (see esp. Chs. i and v, p. 321), and along with Miss Everett's paper (note 57 below) still provides the richest seminal influence.

57. D. Everett, "A Characterization of the English Medieval Romances," *E&S,* XV (1929), 98-121, rptd. in *Essays on Middle English Literature,* ed. P. Kean (Oxford, 1955).·

58. D. M. Hill, "Romance as Epic," *ES,* XLIV (1963), 95-107.

59. Gibbs, M. E. *Romances*, Introd., pp. 20-27; but cf. at p. 22: "romance has to do with the social aura of feudal knighthood, its mores and ideas, with a poem's theme, its meaning, not primarily with its style." Cf. E. Auerbach, *Mimesis* (Berne, Switzerland, 1946; trans. W. Trask, New York, 1957), pp. 107-124; but Pearsall is quite right when he notes that, for the bulk of English romances, adulterous love or feats of arms for their own sake are not the central subject matter. See E. T. Donaldson, "The Myth of Courtly Love," *Ventures*, V (1965), 16-23.

60. John Finlayson, ed., *Morte Arthure*, (Evanston, Ill., 1967) in York Medieval Texts, Introduction, pp. 3-11.

61. Max Wehrli, "Strukturprobleme des mittelalterlichen Romans," *Wirkende Wort*, X (1960), 334-345.

62. D. Mehl: "Die kurzeren mittelenglischen 'Romanzen' und die Gattungsfrage," *DVLG*, XXXVIII (1964), 513-533; " 'Point of View' in mittelenglischen Romanzen," *GRM*, XLV, N.F. 14 (1964), 35-46.

63. D. Pearsall, "The Development of Middle English Romance," *MS*, XXVII (1965), 91-116. All agree on the inadequate and ambiguous nature of classification by subject matter alone. But a definition of a work of art based on who sees or hears it is equally violative of a fundamental canon of criticism. Nykrog has brought the issue to a head by demonstrating the socially and intellectually multi-leveled author-audience for the fabliau. *Quaere* whether the same skepticism should not be applied to our inferences about the authors and audiences of epic and romance. P. Nykrog, *Les Fabliaux*: *Etude d'histoire littéraire et de stylistique médiévale* (Copenhagen, 1957); Jean Rychner, *Contributions a l'étude des fabliaux: Variantes, remaniements, degradations* (2 vols., Geneva, 1960).

64. See R. A. Waldron, "Oral-formulaic Technique in Middle English Alliterative Poetry," *Speculum*, XXXII (1957), 792-804, one of the earliest critiques of the "oral-therefore-formulaic" or "formulaic-therefore-oral" concept; and his M.A. thesis (Univ. of London, 1953): "The Diction of English Alliterative Romances"; also a carefully reasoned and severely critical analysis, with full bibliography, by R. R. Lawrence, "The Formulaic Theory and Its Application to English Alliterative Poetry," in *Essays on Style and Language: Linguistic and Critical Approaches to Literary Style*, ed. Roger Fowler (London, 1966), pp. 166-183; F. G. Cassidy, "How Free Was the Anglo-Saxon Scop?" in *Franciplegius, Medieval and Linguistic Studies in Honor of Francis Peabody Magoun, Jr.*, ed. J. B. Bessinger, Jr., and R. P. Creed (New York, 1965), pp. 75-85; J. Finlayson, ed., *Morte Arthure*, Introd., notes 24-25; M. Bullard, "Some Objections to the Formulaic Theory of the Composition of Anglo-Saxon Narrative Poetry," *Bull. of the Rocky Mt. MLA*, XXI (1967), 11-16. L. Benson, "The Literary Character of Anglo-Saxon Formulaic Poetry," *PMLA*, LXXXI (1966), 334-341; H. L. Rogers, "The Crypto-Psychological Character of the Oral Formula," *ES*, XLVII (1966), 89-102 (bibliog. notes 1-3); D. K. Fry, "Formulas and Systems," *ES*, XLVIII (1967), 193-204 (bibliog. notes 6 ff.) See also Walter J. Ong, S. J., "Oral Residue in Tudor Prose Style," *PMLA*, LXXX (1965), 145-154. The most sophisticated criticism of the method is S. B. Greenfield's "The Canons of Old English Criticism," *ELH*, XXXIV (1967), 141-155.

65. A. C. Baugh: "The Authorship of the Middle English Romances," *The Presidential Address, MHRA: Annual Bulletin No. 22* (1950), pp. 13-28; "Improvisation in the Middle English Romance," *PAPS*, CIII, pt. 3 (June, 1959), 418-454; "The Middle English Romance: Some Questions of Creation, Presentation, and Preservation," *Speculum*, LXII (1967), 1-31. Every critic has been impressed by the strikingly similar verbal

and rhetorical patterns — but each generation sees these through the refractions of its own vision: the early German editors, like Zupitza, Kölbing, Adams, regarded them as proof of sources and borrowings; in the 1930's Trounce and, later, Mrs. L. H. Loomis saw them as evidence of a "school" of "local" poets or of fellow-scribes in a bookshop; in the 1940's C. S. Lewis viewed them as devices catering to the expectations of the audience; in the 1950's similar patterns in OE were urged as proof of spontaneous oral composition for a ready-made metrical-syntactic frame.

66. Michael Curschmann, "Oral Poetry in Medieval English, French, and German Literature: Some Notes on Recent Research," *Speculum*, XLII (January, 1967), 36-52.

67. Alain Renoir, "Imitation, Influence, and Originality," in *Proceedings of the IV Congress of the International Comparative Literature Association, Fribourg 1964*, ed. F. Jost (The Hague, 1966), II, 741.

68. *Preface to Paradise Lost* (London, 1942), p. 19. M. W. Bloomfield, "Understanding Old English Poetry," *AnM*, IX (1968), 5.

69. J. Mitchell, *Thomas Hoccleve: A Study in Early Fifteenth-Century English Poetic* (Urbana, Ill., 1968), pp. 64-67. If the tail-rhyme romances were an aspect of the "bourgeois struggle for self-definition and self-identification" (as Pearsall implies), the Host apparently could not "identify."

70. Larry D. Benson, *Art and Tradition in Sir Gawain and the Green Knight* (New Brunswick, N. J., 1965), p. 119. See Morton W. Bloomfield, *"Piers Plowman* as a Fourteenth-Century Apocalypse," *The Centennial Review*, V (1961), 291: "The medieval writer was very conscious of the kind of form in which he chose to present his artistic vision and . . . it is against the customary lines of this form that we can best understand his innovations and his uniqueness."

71. E. Vinaver, "From Epic to Romance," *BJRL*, XLVI (1964), 476-503; "Critical Approaches to Medieval Romance," in *Literary History and Literary Criticism*, ed. Leon Edel (New York, 1965), pp. 26 ff.; *Form and Meaning in Medieval Romance, The Presidential Address* (Leeds: MHRA, 1966), p. 15. After seventy years of assessing materials and almost as many critical theories, informed thought has come back full circle to Ker's first distinction — definition by comparison and contrast between epic and romance.

72. Phillip Damon, "History and Idea in Renaissance Criticism," in *Literary Criticism and Historical Understanding*, Selected Papers from the English Institute (New York, 1967), pp. 51, 43. Cf. Alfred Foulet, *Speculum*, XLIII (1968), 355: "Romances, because of their freedom from the here and the now, can hardly be coerced into a pattern of compelling logic."

Chaucer's Canterbury Tales

by Helaine Newstead

In 1951 Professor Albert Baugh published in *Speculum*[1] an admirably concise and judicious review of fifty years of Chaucer scholarship. Since that time the volume of Chaucer studies has increased rather than diminished; so much so that anyone who attempts to cover what has been written only about the *Canterbury Tales* will be astonished at its range and diversity. The experience inevitably calls to mind Chaucer's own whirling House of Rumor, though one hopes that some purer form of truth will emerge from the dizzying mass of publication.

I shall not attempt anything like a comprehensive survey, especially since new bibliographical guides by William R. Crawford[2] and Mr. Baugh[3] are readily accessible and reasonably up-to-date. Review articles also appear with considerable frequency. Instead, I shall try to define some distinctive trends and to note the most important issues that have concerned Chaucerians on this side of the Atlantic in recent years.

There can be no doubt that modern Chaucerians are very much aware of their modernity and often somewhat scornful of their predecessors. Chronologically, of course, all of us are post-Romantics and post-Victorians, but these terms have acquired a pejorative sense in the language of the Chaucerian moderns. So, too, have historicism, empiricism, and organicism. We are also warned that we need new critical vocabularies to cope with the literary problems. The new generation, it is true, seeks to answer different questions, chiefly those concerned with interpretation. But the old problems still remain as well as some of the old methods of dealing with them.

Even the most sophisticated of interpreters need editions of the text. Although Robinson's second edition[4] of the complete works still dominates the scene, three new editions of selections from the text have appeared in the past ten years. E. T. Donaldson's edition, *Chaucer's Poetry: An Anthology for the Modern Reader* (New York, 1958), is notable not only for its sensitive literary commentary but also for some new readings. Professor Robert A. Pratt's edition, *Selections from the Tales of Canterbury and Short Poems* (Boston, 1966), also offers interesting new readings, and Professor Baugh's *Chaucer's Major Poetry* (New York, 1963) is distinguished by an unusually full glossary. All four illustrate a perennial problem in the study of the *Canterbury Tales*: the sequence of the tales. Robinson and Donaldson follow the arrangement of the Ellesmere MS, but Baugh and Pratt adopt the order first suggested a hundred years ago by Bradshaw and approved by Skeat. The issue is still debated: Pratt's cogent arguments for the sequence he adopts, first presented in 1951,[5] have been contested by other scholars, but the evidence on either side remains inconclusive.

This is a period in Chaucer scholarship in which biographical and historical studies, at least in the United States, are held in

low esteem. A significant landmark, nevertheless, is the publication of the new edition of the *Life-Records* in 1966[6] by Profes-
sors Crow and Olson. This monumental work is really a legacy
from an earlier generation since it was initiated by Manly and
Rickert nearly forty years before its eventual publication, but it
would never have been completed without the dedicated labors of
the present editors. Although not directly concerned with the
Canterbury Tales, it reminds us that the poet was also a public
servant, a widely travelled man of affairs, a diplomat and a
courtier — a fact easy to forget if one reads much current
criticism.

The new editions and the *Life-Records,* important though
they are, represent peripheral interests today. Recent treatments
of the *Canterbury Tales* have been subject to the main tendencies in Chaucer scholarship and criticism, which in general center
upon the religious and intellectual background rather than the
historical. Modern studies have also been fruitful in exploring
aspects of style and rhetoric in fresh ways that illuminate and
define the qualities of Chaucer's art. Iconography, architecture,
and other non-verbal arts have also been studied in the effort to
reach the principles of the Chaucerian aesthetic.

Ralph Baldwin's monograph, *The Unity of the Canterbury
Tales,* first published in 1955,[7] has had an extraordinary influence, perhaps because some of its most persuasive arguments
have been widely circulated in the anthology compiled by
Schoeck and Taylor in 1960.[8] At least before that time it seems
to have attracted little notice as it reposed in the pages of
Anglistica. Baldwin's study emphasizes the religious significance
of the pilgrimage as the dominant metaphor of the planned
structure, and devotes close attention to a hitherto neglected section, the *Parson's Tale.* By developing the religious implications
of the pilgrimage, he is able to show, to the satisfaction of many

Chaucerians, that the theme of penitence typical of pilgrimages unifies the General Prologue and the *Parson's Tale.* His effort to link the pilgrims and their tales to the sins denounced in the *Parson's Tale* has been less successful. His eloquent analysis of the General Prologue in terms of medieval rhetorical theory and practice has been as influential as his rehabilitation of the *Parson's Tale* and has stimulated others to pursue further studies in the same direction.

Baldwin's monograph exemplifies both major tendencies in modern Chaucerian criticism: the two R's of Religion and Rhetoric. The most massive and controversial work dealing with the religious and intellectual background, however, is D. W. Robertson's *A Preface to Chaucer* (Princeton, 1962). It is a storehouse of information about the methods of scriptural exegesis, medieval iconography, and Augustinian literary theory, in support of the author's major thesis that all medieval literature, including the secular, was governed by the single aim of teaching charity in its largest religious sense and rejecting its opposite, cupidity. The controversy, for those who are interested and still unfamiliar with it, may be followed in the review articles by F. L. Utley, R. E. Kaske, William Matthews, R. O. Payne, C. L. Wrenn, among others.[9] These are conveniently listed in the exegesis of Robertson's theories by A. Leigh DeNeef published in the *Chaucer Review,*[10] which should also be consulted. Most opponents would admit the importance of exegetical material as part of the intellectual background but would deny it the central place in the foreground of literary studies claimed for it by Robertson. Medieval culture is far more diversified and dissonant than the theory allows, and the exclusion of other traditions and tendencies limits its critical value. The application of the theory to the *Canterbury Tales* results in some strained interpretations that distort rather than illuminate the text. Despite these short-

comings, there is rich value in the detailed study of the icono-
graphic tradition and in the copious and learned commentary
on theological doctrine.

The second major interest among modern Chaucerians is style,
rhetoric, and medieval aesthetic theory, represented in three note-
worthy books. The earliest and most influential is Charles Muscatine's *Chaucer and the French Tradition* (Berkeley and Los
Angeles, 1957). Subtitled "A Study in Style and Meaning," it
examines style as an essential component of meaning, distinguishing in the French tradition inherited by Chaucer two kinds
of style, one typical of the romance, the other of the fabliau.
More than half the book is devoted to an analysis of French style
and its application to the dream visions and *Troilus*. Although
the treatment of the *Canterbury Tales* is neither complete nor
central, it is systematic. Muscatine established juxtaposition as
the characteristic of Gothic art that best explains the larger form
of the work, the linear sequence of independent stories in various
styles. Within the individual tales there is also a mixture of
styles. In his detailed study of eight tales, he distinguishes the two
stylistic conventions, although the terms he uses, courtly and
bourgeois, imply a social distinction that is not supported by
recent studies of the fabliau.[11] The analysis of the tales reveals
with sensitivity and imagination the range of Chaucer's style,
not only his mastery of the two inherited conventions but also
his brilliant manipulation of what Muscatine terms the "mixed"
style. These important insights are more fully developed in his
later essay, "The Canterbury Tales: Style of the Man and Style
of the Work," published in 1966,[12] in a volume of critical essays
edited by D. S. Brewer.

Muscatine's studies touch, when required, upon problems of
rhetoric. A re-examination of rhetoric and medieval poetic theory
is the subject of Robert O. Payne's book, *The Key of Remem-*

brance (New Haven, Conn., 1963). The single chapter on the *Canterbury Tales,* the author informs us (p. 8), is to be read as a supplement to Baldwin's conclusions. Although the tales receive comparatively little attention in this book, the thoughtful reconsideration of medieval poetic theory as it was understood and used by Chaucer shows that it was no mechanical application of rules but rather a difficult concept of serious art that led to various kinds of experimentation. In the light of Payne's admittedly incomplete but challenging analysis, Chaucer appears not only as a master of the established literary conventions but also as an experimental poet aware of the major problems in the art of poetry. The questions posed though not always answered in Payne's book suggest prospects for further exploration.

A different approach to aesthetic problems is presented in Robert M. Jordan's *Chaucer and the Shape of Creation* (Cambridge, Mass., 1967). The subtitle, "The Aesthetic Possibilities of Inorganic Structure," suggests one of its major theses: that it is futile to expect organic unity in medieval art since the underlying concept is quantitative and inorganic. Drawing upon analogies with the structural principles of the Gothic cathedral, he finds that Chaucer's narrative art is aggregative, not organic; the structural elements are coordinate and separable units, juxtaposed in various ways and with various effects. He applies this thesis to the structural features of six of the tales to account for the presence of discordant elements, discontinuities, lapses of style, breaking of fictional illusion, and other irregularities troublesome to believers in organic unity. The arguments also challenge other conventional attitudes towards the tales, especially the concept of dramatic structure, the assumption of a close relationship of tale to teller, of purposefully developed characterization, and the significance of the narrator and the nature of his audience. The chief casualty seems to be the idea of roadside drama, first

102

developed by Kittredge and amplified by later critics. But although the book stresses inconsistencies, abrupt shifts, and other discords, it does not deny unity. It is the framework of pilgrimage and the thematic relevance of the *Parson's Tale* that establish what he calls a "multiple unity," in which the autonomous elements are held together within the dominant outline. The book presents a comprehensive theory about the principles of Chaucerian structure, but its validity needs to be tested in a fuller range of narrative.

A less controversial book is Paul Ruggiers' *The Art of the Canterbury Tales*, published two years before Jordan's.[13] Accepting, like Jordan, Baldwin's conclusions about the metaphorical significance of the pilgrimage as frame, he studies the tales themselves, concentrating upon theme and genre rather than structure and analyzing the techniques of what he terms "the medley." The tales are difficult to classify, but he groups the most important of them (fifteen in all) into two categories: comic tales and romances, examining them from the point of view of Chaucer's moral vision. Although his study demonstrates the diversity of human experience in the tales rather than the unity which he seeks in them as in the framework, the book offers informed and thoughtful readings of the individual tales and links.

Time does not permit consideration of other important books and studies that have appeared in recent years. It should be noted, in passing, that the role of the pilgrim-narrator continues to be a topic of lively discussion marked by differing but not necessarily incompatible points of view, as Donald Howard has shown in his article "Chaucer the Man."[14] One noticeable trend in the enormous output of articles is the focus upon tales ignored or neglected in earlier commentary. The *Manciple's Tale*, the *Second Nun's Tale*, the *Canon's Yoeman's Tale*, the *Summoner's Tale* have all been examined in recent studies as never before.

New interpretations of the more familiar tales, of course, continue to proliferate. Many of these articles are valuable, but the eccentricities of others move one to sympathize with the gloomy exasperation expressed by J. Burke Severs in a recent essay. Let me quote: "... the duty of the critic to keep his eye on the poem and to seek to understand and appreciate it as in itself it *is*, is no longer recognized by many modern critics. They do not hesitate to falsify the emphases in a poem, to import into their reading foreign and external considerations, to allow modern attitudes to displace medieval and to impose irrelevant medieval attitudes, to permit private, idiosyncratic, supersubtle interpretations to replace the natural and obvious. This has led to absurd and perverse judgments. Accordingly, much of what is being written these days in Chaucer criticism is invalid: the sufficient answer to most of it is simply to reread the poem carefully."[15]

Since the *Canterbury Tales* exist in a fragmentary state, it is natural to seek order and to find it, to overlook discrepancies, and to fill in gaps. If some tales are clearly linked to their tellers, it is easy to assume that all must have been planned to reveal the personalities of the pilgrims, whatever may be the present state of the text. This view, familiar in earlier criticism, leads to a disproportionate emphasis upon the pilgrims, and to the implication that the tales are extensions of their characters. Modern criticism has been salutary in modifying such assumptions by directing attention to the discontinuities of the text and to such signs of external adjustment as the shifts of some tales to different tellers. It is well, too, to be reminded that the *Canterbury Tales* are fiction. On the other hand, modern critics, liberated from Kittredge and his disciples, tend to exaggerate the independence of the fragments and to construct theories based on only those tales that support them. The modernist approach also suffers from a failure to consider alternative explanations. Many of the peculiarities of

Chaucerian narrative technique, for instance, can be explained in terms of composition for oral presentation. The oral aspect of Chaucer's art may have been overestimated in the past since it is obvious that the poet also had in mind other audiences than the one immediately present. But the public nature of poetry in Chaucer's time is too significant to be overlooked; it may not explain everything, but it is surely not irrelevant.

The recent explorations into the intellectual, theological, and aesthetic backgrounds of Chaucer's poetry can indeed be instructive. But the most rewarding area, it seems to me, is the study of Chaucer's concepts of the art of poetry. The pioneer work of Muscatine, Donaldson,[16] and Payne in Chaucerian stylistics and poetics suggests the value of such an approach. Much remains to be done in the study of Chaucer's style, rhetoric, literary language, and prosody, and the results should be enlightening.

The poet who emerges from most of the recent commentary on the *Canterbury Tales* is a solemn figure dominated by the *Parson's Tale* and its terrifying shadows, a poet for the Age of Anxiety. This forbidding apparition should not obliterate the more familiar poet whose joy in the created world and its fallible inhabitants has delighted generations of readers. The problems arising from the unfinished, fragmentary state of the *Canterbury Tales* will continue to suggest new solutions. One must always return to the text, and learn to distinguish between interpretations that deepen or expand our understanding and those that restrict it to fit a preconceived theory. Chaucer seems to be the most accessible of poets, but, as all thoughtful critics soon realize, he is also one of the most elusive.

Notes

1. Albert C. Baugh, "Fifty Years of Chaucer Scholarship," *Speculum*, XXVI (1951), 659-672.

2. William R. Crawford, *Bibliography of Chaucer, 1954-63* (Seattle, London, 1967).

3. A. C. Baugh, *Chaucer*, Goldentree Bibliographies (New York, 1968).

4. *The Works of Geoffrey Chaucer*, ed. F. N. Robinson (2nd edn., Boston, 1957).

5. Robert A. Pratt, "The Order of the *Canterbury Tales*," *PMLA*, LXVI (1951), 1141-1167.

6. *Chaucer Life-Records*, ed. Martin M. Crow, Clair C. Olson (Oxford, 1966).

7. *Anglistica*, V (Copenhagen, 1955).

8. *Chaucer Criticism, The Canterbury Tales: An Anthology*, ed. Richard J. Schoeck, Jerome Taylor (Notre Dame, Ind., 1960), pp. 14-51.

9. F. L. Utley, "Robertsonianism Redivivus," *RPh*, XIX (1965), 250-260; R. E. Kaske, "Chaucer and Medieval Allegory," *ELH*, XXX (1963), 175-192; William Matthews, *RPh*, XVII (1964), 638-542; Robert O. Payne, *CL*, XV (1963), 269-271; C. L. Wrenn, *JEGP*, LXII (1963), 794-801.

10. A. Leigh DeNeef, "Robertson and the Critics," *Chaucer Review*, II (1968), 205-234.

11. Per Nykrog, *Les Fabliaux* (Copenhagen, 1957).

12. *Chaucer and Chaucerians, Critical Studies in Middle English Literature*, ed. D. S. Brewer (London, 1966), pp. 88-113.

13. Paul G. Ruggiers, *The Art of the Canterbury Tales* (Madison and Milwaukee, Wis., 1965).

14. *PMLA*, LXXX (1965), 337-343.

15. J. Burke Severs, "The Tales of Romance," *Companion to Chaucer Studies*, ed. Beryl Rowland (Oxford, 1968), p. 240.

16. E. T. Donaldson, "Idiom of Popular Poetry in the *Miller's Tale*," *English Institute Essays, 1950* (New York, 1951), pp. 116-140. (Reprinted in *Chaucer and His Contemporaries, Essays on Medieval Literature and Thought*, ed. Helaine Newstead [New York, 1968], pp. 174-189).